NLP: How you can get the best out of yourself and others using Neuro-Linguistic Programming the right way

I0428761

By Thomas D Edison

Table of Contents

Chapter 1

Introduction

We are all looking for ways to understand how we work. It is our nature to think about thinking, but sometimes it gives us a headache because the rabbit hole is very, very deep. This book will hopefully give you a better understanding of how and why you react a certain way through looking at how language and expression can influence you, just as Morgan Freeman's voice makes some people go silly. Neuro-Linguistic Programming can help shed some light on why we are more musical than arty or how we can use language more efficiently and to better effect. Why waste your breath on a one-hundred-word phrase when five words will get your point across better and more to the point, it will stick. If you stick with it, you will improve your chances at achieving what you need to achieve, because you will learn how to break things down to the raw components.

What is Neuro-Linguistic Programming?

Neuro-Linguistic Programming is a psycholinguistic model that can help build rapport, change opinions, plant ideas, overcome mental disorders and facilitate personal growth amongst other beneficial functional uses, according to its creators Bandler and Grinder (1976). It is based on the idea that behavior can be altered or influenced through manipulation of neurological processes, all of which are connected to linguistic representations in the verbal store in the long term memory and in the phonological loop where language is silently rearticulated in the working memory. It sounds like a magical miracle cure for deep-set, difficult to treat psychological conditions, but is it all top hats and bunny rabbits? It is largely dependent on other theories that refer to the unconscious mind as a powerful tool such as Erickson's work on medical hypnotherapy and Gestalt therapists' perceptions of how people achieve a positive mind frame. Because of this it is impossible to unequivocally assess its usability. But it has been tested under controlled conditions and has yielded surprising results which seem to support the notion that it is helping people to better process difficult to digest information and achieve personal goals.

What are the problems?

There is a huge debate over whether it should be taken seriously or not. Counter theorists say there is nowhere near enough quantitative or qualitative data to make such wild claims. Supporting theorists claim that the results that they have complied are evidences in itself of the functionality of NLP. So it is experiential research that is the driving force behind the NLP model. It is not going to escape pseudoscientific status whilst the supporting evidence is so thin but it has proven to be a useful tool for a great many circumstances. And that was all it was intended to be. A mental model will always stumble over irregularities because the mind is a phenomenon yet to be fully understood so we can't apply limiting factors to fully control experiments. If we take a positivist stance however, and consider the regularities as meaningful (which they usually are) then we may just make some headway (Bandler, and Grinder, 1976).

You may have heard of various Neuro-Linguistic Programming techniques such as lie detection by tracking eye movement. The one that claims that if someone is looking up and to the right, he or she is lying, up to the left and it is the truth. There is some logic behind this idea, as it refers to the eyes gazing into the part of the brain that is responsible for memories or creations, but it's unlikely that many would use this technique when sniffing out a cheater as there are just too many ifs and buts surrounding it. The problem with NLP techniques is that there is little empirical evidence to support the model which they use, just a whole lot of people demonstrating its usefulness. The creators themselves, Bandler and Grinder openly made a point of this issue when they presented their findings by stating that they are not 'psychologists, theologians or theoreticians'; they have 'no idea about the true nature of mental representations' and they are 'not interested in proving their theory'. But that didn't stop a new wave of psychologists, neurologists, linguists and anthropologists creating a quasi-religion dedicated to exploring and developing the model that Bandler and Grinder came up with. And they came up with some good stuff (Bandler, R and Grinder, J, 1976).

How can you use it?

NLP has such overwhelming support from different fields of study because the applications for NLP are infinite. It is up to the enthusiasts to prove its worth as a standalone theory, independent of other, more renowned works by testing it as a vague hypothesis in situations where language can be used to influence behavior.

In therapy, psychotherapists have used NLP techniques to reach their patients on an unconscious level in order to make lasting changes in their psyche. As knowingly accepting psychotherapeutic techniques could be counterproductive due to the emergence of counterarguments against the treatment, it is important for patients to be in an open and malleable state of mind. Psychotherapists have NLP tricks up their sleeve that help make patients more susceptible to their influence as well as techniques based on the model to 'talk to' their patients' subconscious. Such problems as phobias, family feuds, anxiety and depression are but a handful of potential aspects where NLP can be of use and lasting change is an area in which NLP seems to be particularly helpful. Change in patients' way of harmful thinking is demonstrated in other techniques such as exposure and positive association to a stimulus, but with techniques of

NLP there is notable longevity of change. Patients are less likely to return to the self-detrimental behavior if they are affected on an unconscious level because they aren't directly aware of how the change has happened and thusly cannot undo it. There are however limitations when using NLP in a psychotherapeutic context as it depends largely on the psychiatrist's ability and the patient's willingness to commit to the treatment. In extreme cases of trauma for instance, a patient is required to recall the painful experience that caused the trauma in order to get better, but in some of these cases the trauma is so severe that a patient will continue to repress the memory rather than recall it, continuing the cycle of internal torture.

Similar to the way psychiatrists use NLP to influence the change of a negative behavior pattern, advertising agencies use NLP to prey on the unconscious mind of the consumer in order to get them to buy their product. Enter the darker side of Neuro-Linguistic Programming. Where one can bend another's will with mild suggestive action or plant an idea unbeknown to the interlocutor. This has been born out of the constant need for fresh marketing techniques as capitalism grows exponentially. In traditional advertising, most of the focus was rather one sided, highlighting all the positive factors of a product. But over time, as the public responded better to more rounded, less biased, entertaining adverts, advertising agencies were forced to up their game and develop new techniques such as those of NLP in order to compete with rival brands, who sold pretty much the same product which usually suffered from the same downfalls. Rather than focusing on the vibrant color schemes that famously attract a younger audience, NLP in advertising focuses on the captions and slogans of the brand, as well as the dialogue in some cases. They cleverly 'reframe' a potential pitfall of the product as a 'desirable' attribute under the right circumstances. The audience is invited to look past the negative and consider the beneficial aspects of having to deal with a prevalent feature obviously detrimental to the product image.

Another common circumstance in which NLP techniques are used is in the classroom. Teachers and students alike appear to have benefited from the use of rapport building techniques that the power relation between them necessitates. And especially in exam situations when all manner of breathing techniques, rituals and praying are executed with pure anxiety as the root cause, teachers that incorporate NLP techniques in their lessons are not only able to gauge the dominant learning style of the students, be it visual, auditory or kinesthetic, they are also able to pass that information on to the students themselves, directing their efforts to use a learning style tailor made for their own needs. One of the models that are similar to NLP is the Multiple Intelligence model, which states that there are eight different types of intelligence which each of us possess with varying levels of ability. Whilst the NLP model only employs three hypernymic categories, both models agree that people have one of these methods as their preferred means of cognition and so should focus on that particular aspect when learning whilst aiming to improve their other 'intelligences' separately.

In competitive sports, the element of deception is all too common; just ask any football player who has played against Ronaldinho. Similarly, in a court of criminal law, one party is being deceitful in an effort to win the case. Both situations are set in a hugely competitive environment, making it highly likely that temperatures will be high and the truth will be difficult to ascertain. NLP techniques can be manipulated to help the deceiver, as the rapport building techniques could quite easily be abused by gaining someone's trust only to later throw them under the bus. But whereas this may work in an uncompetitive environment, in competition, people expect others to play a little dirty. Jurors should be aware of the persuasive tactics such as NLP that lawyers may use. Teammates could use NLP to help with team spirit. But equally, they could use it to feign left and go right, just like a lawyer does in court.

The rise of the internet and technology has caused the world to stop what they were doing, and pick up a keyboard. With that, the desire to create things more complex has naturally followed and we are now at the stage where we may have new robot companions to share our world with, so we had better learn their language in order to chat with them. The only problem is that they speak a language far more complicated than ancient Hungarian, so it may be easier just to teach them ours. The machines need some guidance on how to become fully autonomous, heuristic beings. We can give it to them if we dare. Through the magic of neuro-linguistic programming and neuro-fuzzy systems. We tell them what to do and how to do it, give them some rules to follow, and watch the algorithm give life to a circuit-board.

When communicating in relationships, it is important not to step on too many toes; otherwise you may end up in the dog house. Couples can use NLP techniques to better understand one another through building rapport and arguing more constructively as opposed to getting frustrated with one another. Parents could also use stress reducing techniques to control how they act in front of young children, as getting angry often causes children to model the negative behavior. Whilst generally healthy relationships do not need any intervention, it can be useful to gain an understanding of how certain words may affect other people, like how honing in on people's inner most insecurities can hurt people, even if it was meant as a joke. A better understanding of social behavior leads to less awkward moments and better conversation. Don't be the awkward one.

Chapter 2

Education

Perhaps some of the best research on NLP has been done with regard to education as the building of rapport between teacher and student and dealing with the emotions of students in class is something that most teachers seem to struggle with at least from time to time. There is also the difficulty of attending to the learners' educational needs in a way that is conducive to their particular style. Teachers so often don't have training in this aspect of their job which is arguably the most important part. If the learning environment is not one in which students may feel comfortable in opening up, letting their barriers down, disengaging the frontal cortex and subsequently allowing for better absorption of material, then the teacher has failed at his job before he has started. Prominent NLP techniques may be used in the classroom such as reframing and collapsing anchors to achieve this so called 'Zone of Congruence'. If students are not achieving desired results, and the C-Zone appears to be working fine, a teacher may reframe the subject matter in a way that is easier to understand. If the student is still struggling after this, a teacher may have to resort to discovering why that is. In this capacity she may draw on such NLP techniques as collapsing an anchor which can help students to overcome previous mental blocks or anchors. As the C-Zone is so important with the implication of NLP techniques in teaching due to it being the state in which students are most receptive, maintaining it must also be a priority. If that means counselling, reassuring or motivating a student then teachers must have the skill set to do that.

There are many different students with many different personalities, each one of them with a preferred learning style. The level of the learners will also require the teacher to adapt his or her style. There are probably another hundred or so factors that the teacher has to take into account in order to get the most positive response out of his or her students individually as generally, the more positive the lesson is, the better it will be understood because everyone likes to draw on positive memories. One common way to build rapport is to mimic the actions of another. It is human nature to mirror what others are doing as we all have built in Mirror Neurons which serve that very purpose. Likewise, deviation from the actions of others is considered to be rude. It implies that one is trying to distance himself from another. It would appear easy for teachers to mimic the behavior of students in order to gain their focus and attention, but as you may have noticed, it isn't. Overdoing it is the most common crime when mimicking others' behavior as it can seem unnatural and forced. If convergent behavior does not appear at least partially one's own, then it can appear offensive, or in the case of a student and teacher, 'super cringe'. How then does one build a meaningful connection with someone of a different generation when a power relative situation is forced on them? As with most things, it comes down to attitude. If a teacher uses a nonchalant approach whilst teaching whilst teaching for instance, he won't be influencing interest in his students, so he is not doing his job. If the teacher is overly excited however, he is probably not accommodating his level of enthusiasm to that of the students. The teacher needs to strike a balance somewhere between the two. This comes by way of careful deliberation of the individual learners' personalities. As the teacher gets to know her students individually, she can start to come up with teaching methods that suit the class as a whole and then adopt new methods to focus on individuals when necessary. If only the former is done, it leads to the outdated 'sage on the stage' model of teaching, in which the teacher is performing to the students and not communicating with them. If there is no element of reciprocation, there can be no 'cybernetic loop' and henceforth the learning process ceases to be dynamic and reduces to nothing more than background noise. Incidentally, a good time to use the NLP concept of idea placement as the unconscious mind is being addressed. But when learning calculus, it won't help much if you only rely on a tingling sensation in your amygdala that you have the correct answer. You need your working memory focused on a subject in order to send it to the long term memory. Unconscious memories are stored in the amygdala which are affected by such chemicals as dopamine as they are normally emotional memories. Not a good place to store maths as they appear as vague, sensory representations but perhaps you could send a more basic message like, "do your homework or die". Conscious memories on the other hand are stored in the hippocampus and can be reasoned with and rehearsed thereby strengthening the memory and subjecting it to logical debate and creative solutions. A teacher needs to simultaneously exact the target material on the students' working memory and stimulate the amygdala, so that a positive association is made between the two systems. It is a very simple reward system when you look at it like this, hence why candy is perhaps one of the best tools for primary school teachers. But as we get older we look for new dopamine highs so it gets a little more complicated for teachers. They can't very well offer cigarettes to students as rewards to create that positive association, that would be forcing it, not to mention, irresponsible and probably illegal.

In the classroom

The focus of NLP is not so much on the linguistic aspect in the context of a classroom. The concept of using specific words and phrases to better impart knowledge from teacher to student has been around for some time and portrays NLP as a very narrow, easy to master set of principles that can help students. One basic method that has been used since the discovery of NLP in the seventies is the regulation of modal operators such as 'should', 'ought to', 'must' and 'have to' as these auxiliary verbs can imply there is a definitively correct answer and that the students' wrong answer is useless, when really it is a natural part of the learning process to make mistakes (Andreas, 2000). The broader perspective suggests that there is more to NLP than simply using 'trigger' words to achieve the desired effect, in this case the retention of information. Instead a teacher must use a combination of language and expression to allow the student to reach a more authentic concordance with the teacher. One disciple of Bandler and Grinder notes that after a teacher has correctly assessed the preferred learning means, or 'sensory modality' of a student, he can then accommodate his teaching style to that of the student's by using a style of language conducive to that student's learning medium i.e. visual, auditory or kina esthetic (Brockopp, 1983). Some of the key words that Brockopp exhorts teachers to use are 'see', 'listen' and 'feel' relative to their respective hypernymic categories. In a conversation with a student who prefers learning visually for example, a teacher may use these phrases;

"I *see* what the problem is"

"Show your working"

"You *appear* to have changed"

"Are we *clear*"

"Look it up dammit!"

This triggers a focus on the visual aspects or a representation of a concept visually. Likewise, when using the auditory sensory medium, a teacher should focus and refer to sounds and phonological representations through use of phrases such as;

"Do you like how that *sounds*?"

"I *hear* you were expelled"

"It's just going in one *ear* and out the other"

"Don't take that *tone* with me bub"

"Listen up dammit!"

And with students inclined to learn kinaesthetically, whilst there are not as many teaching methods that support this in most subjects other than physical education (largely because it requires more effort) a teacher can still animate her teaching style by using 'doing' words in dynamic, perhaps metaphorical phrases like for instance;

"You are *holding* your head up high today"

"Your *grasp* of the content has *impressed* me"

"*Write* that down if you can't *remember* it"

"Do you *feel* that you did well?"

"*Think* dammit!"

Hopefully by recognizing and accommodating to the learner's preferred medium of learning the teacher will have gained the pupil's respect in one form or another as it gives the impression that the teacher is not just doing his job, he is actively trying to engage with the student on a personal level. Equally, in a classroom with lots of students where it is not always possible to talk to each student individually, appealing to all three of these key senses methodically and intermittently will appeal to the whole class.

The argument against this technique however is that it is still a technique and therefore it creates unnatural rapport between student and teacher that can't be sustained. But we all use proven social structures when getting to know people, so what's the big difference? This rapport building technique helps put both parties on the same wavelength, which can be difficult when the relationship implies a distinct power imbalance (Andreas, 2000). This accommodation technique could potentially backfire if the trust is broken between the two as using a technique such as this in order to gain trust is a total paradox. But when students are in the C-Zone (the zone of congruence) their defences are down, leading them to be less vigilant of potential manipulation the same way that hypnotists can freely mess with people once they are hypnotized. Teachers are generally not sociopaths and so one would hope that they'd use these techniques for good rather than to get students to bring them a cup of coffee every lesson. What helps this is a bond between student and teacher which is best achieved through good old shared information. This nurtures trust and allows a relationship to continue being one in which information is absorbed rather than repelled. A heuristic approach is often employed by teachers who consider themselves as mere facilitators of learning. The goals for a teacher who uses this approach are to get out of the way when necessary and to allow a student to ponder at will. This, coupled with empathy is a powerful combination as the student is under the impression that the teacher is not actually teaching, he's guiding. And that is a much more acceptable function in a relationship because it can be demoralizing to take the insinuation that you can't come up with the answer yourself as is the case in the typical classroom of old where a teacher would be used to asserting authority over his students. This modern, communicative approach is generally speaking accepted by students because it gets them to think of the answer so they are the instigators, not the teacher, who is sat on the side-lines acting as a friendly guide who has been there and done it. Another technique derived from NLP that can be used to achieve this desirable, inclusive classroom mentality is 'pacing', referring to the continuation of the train of thought of the learner by the teacher, thereby solidifying the importance of the objective thinking of the student even if the idea is partly misunderstood. In this instance, rectifications can be suggested to make the point better rather than focusing on the errors. If a student gives a very open ended question, a good reply might be, "that's a very novel idea," rather than plainly negative feedback such as, "I don't think that is relevant to the topic." It may sound like too much nurturing to some people, but the mind is fragile and one knock off balance could be the 'anchor' that stops a student from trying a second time. The collapsing of an anchor such as this is not easily achieved as it requires reverse engineering, thinking back to the time when the anchor was made and then reframing it in a positive light by using a different way to explain it. Teachers frequently come across students who have suffered negative feedback prior to meeting them, but they don't know how to help them overcome the trauma. It is a difficult process because to be successful it requires not only a strong rapport with the student, the student needs to open up about his or her problem and to get to that stage requires sometimes Zen-like patience on behalf of the teacher in order to unravel the root cause. Because teachers are often so preoccupied with the overall performance of a class, they often don't have time for each and every problem child in the class, but techniques of NLP could be a more efficient way of dealing with them. Teachers also unknowingly (or even knowingly) leave students behind when not enough attention is being payed to the emotional wellbeing of the individual. This is a worrying mentality unwelcome in schools but is still a problem amongst students who go home with little or no understanding of a topic and come in the next day to find that the class has moved on to a different subject. Leaving them with gaps that they will have to rectify themselves without any sort of direction. The best way to teach teachers on how to look after their students and make sure they are not falling behind would be to introduce this concept and other NLP based ideals, but PGCE programs don't generally take much of an interest in them and Master's courses in education are not that popular in the UK. In Finland however, one of the most impressive educational systems in the world, teachers must possess a Master's degree in their area of study or one similar to it. This has led to their impressive school system in which teachers only teach on average, three and a half hours of the day. They do however, in their free time go and sit in on their peers' lessons and make notes which can help both themselves and their colleagues improve their technique. Teaching is a revered occupation in Finland and has been for some time, so is taken very seriously by students and teachers alike. It goes to show that quality over quantity is the way to go in education which is gained from the use of such techniques as reframing, rapport building, election of sensory modality and pacing to name a few.

Teaching Languages

A particular area where NLP techniques are useful is in teaching another language when the teacher does not speak the native language of the student. This is because the language that is used is not easily understood so the expressions of the teacher are the most important tool of communication. In an environment of communicative language teaching (CLT), micro and macro expressions are given particular attention as they are used by teachers consciously and unconsciously, letting the students know or giving them a better idea of the intended message. In language teaching, macro expressions are more useful as they can serve to anchor good and bad behavior, whilst micro expressions can lead to confusion, especially when there are cultural norms that the teacher uses and the student doesn't understand them. There have been lots of studies in this area because the results are so consistent. One such study focuses on the motivational aspect of English Language Lessons given by a British teacher to Iranian students. The motivation of the students and the resulting proficiency of their language was tested. This was a qualitative study so there were only two groups tested. The control group was taught by the English teacher who used his own techniques and scripts whilst the other group was taught by the same teacher but he was given a script and techniques that centered around techniques of NLP. The results before and after the introduction of NLP are shown in the data below;

"An independent-samples t-test was conducted to compare the attitude scores of motivation as a pre-test. There was no significant difference in scores for NLP class (M=13.33, SD=6.00) and traditional class (M=12.70, SD=5.08649; t (98) =.441, p=.11 (two tailed). The magnitude of the differences in the means mean difference=.63, 95% CI: .63 to 3.51)".

"An independent-samples t-test was conducted to compare scores of motivation as a post test. There was a significant difference in scores between NLP class (M=23.03, SD=2.73) and traditional class (M= 12.70, SD= 5.08649; t (98) = -.069, p=.11 (two tailed). The magnitude of the differences in the means (mean difference= 10.33, 95% CI: 10.33 to 12.45)"

Lashkarian, 2015

The study found that the students were more motivated after the lesson which incorporated the NLP techniques and as a result, their language proficiency was notably greater than that of the control class afterwards. The comments from the teacher showed that the students were more actively involved and because of this they enjoyed the class more. The teacher assessed this by referring to the initial limiting factors of the test which grouped the students into the three sensory modality categories, visual, auditory and kinaesthetic and then through observing the changes in kinaesthetic learners' involvement. The NLP techniques helped stop the kinaesthetic learners twiddling their pencils and got them to repeat what the teacher was saying and doing. The teacher achieved this by first mirroring some of the mannerisms of the students, and then after they had relaxed a little because of this they started to reciprocate and followed the macro expressions and language of the teacher. It is a good example of how NLP promotes the imitation and modelling of behavior to give students another learning outlet, one which in this case is preferred by many of the more physically orientated students. But it is not limited to kinaesthetic learners because auditory and visual learners are also encouraged to rehearse the actions of the teacher, be they expressions or speech, in either the Visio-Spatial Sketchpad for visual learners or the Phonological Loop for auditory learners. The focus was on providing a variety of learning mediums and modelling of the teacher's behavior.

Fatigue in school

Fatigue has been colored as distracting, debilitating and potentially dangerous in cases such as driving, so it was something that researchers felt they had to examine. In the context of a high school classroom it can be especially useful as teenagers need as much sleep as babies and can get cranky if they are not left to lie in on the weekend. Couple that with a body that has just started to sprout hair and puss...there are enough distractions for teenagers at school.

Chronic Fatigue Syndrome (CFS) is a common disorder amongst teenagers. It is estimated that about one in fifty have it worldwide, with the majority of sufferers in their teens. CFS came to light at the time ME was first discovered and it was labelled as a similar type of inhibiting disease as it could similarly cause physiological, cognitive, behavioral, affective, and social problems. CFS shares common risk markers with other functional somatic syndromes, but it has been hypothesized by some researchers and clinicians to be a discrete functional somatic syndrome that is made up of different sub-phenotypes (White, 2010). It is not a disease that can be treated medically, although there are pills such as antidepressant and Xanax that can help short term, so there needs to be psychiatric intervention for any lasting change to be made. This commonly comes in the form of Cognitive Behavior Therapy. CBT is a similar method to NLP in that it focuses on modifying the brain's thought patterns so that the chemical imbalance stops stress inducing hormones from being sent to the amygdala. The common techniques associated with CBT include maintaining cycles, mind-body links, goal setting, exploration of helpful and unhelpful thought processes and 'homework' to practice outside of sessions (Parker, 2011). CBT and NLP meet each other at the 'Lighting Process'. This hybrid treatment draws on techniques from both models of experimental psychiatry. The first thing that advocates of the Lighting Process teach is the Physical Emergency Response (PER) which refers to, "the body's natural response to a threat and involves activation of the sympathetic nervous system along with production of hormones such as adrenaline, nor adrenaline, dopamine, cortisol, and DHEA. Although a good way of temporarily dealing with threats, the PER could have detrimental effects on different body systems if sustained. This includes disruption of the immune system, the muscular system, the digestive system, and the nervous system" (Reme et. al, 2012). It can therefore be not only dangerous to others when driving or damaging in cognition, it can actively harm your health. Furthermore, it could lead to more serious mental illness which manifest from such debilitating conditions as fatigue, depression and anxiety. The PER has, at its roots, a 'Physiological Catch 22' which is similar to an anchor in NLP depicting a negative event that seems at first to be a supressed memory that influences future inhibitory actions. With the help of the Lighting Process however one may destabilize physiological catch 22 and stop it from initiating the sympathetic nervous system which leads the sufferer into a downward spiral of self-doubt and giving up on personal goals amongst other harmful ways of thinking. Whilst there have been few clinical trials of the Lighting Process, it has had documented success amongst sufferers who claim that they have used techniques to trick their brain into thinking that everything is peachy and they would be a fool not to love life. One of the most successful of these techniques was the 'power pose'. This is proving to be popular at the moment as you may have come across an article on how one doctor gets up in the morning, makes herself as big as she can possibly make herself, and holds that pose for a minute every morning. Because her posture is confident and her pose powerful, she in turn feels like she is confident. It goes on to suggest that such an empowering posture should be used in the office or the classroom where varying degrees of power exist and can trick people into thinking that you are confident. It is no cliché that even if you aren't confident that pretending to be is the best way to achieve it.

The Lighting Process has been tested in very few controlled situations but one qualitative study aimed to discover how both the affected students and their parents felt about the treatment, so there was a first and third person viewpoint. These interviews lasted anywhere from ten minutes to one hour depending on the length of the answers given. The students were approached in an empathetic manner as their condition may have been worsened by stressful conditions and the test was to aimed at gauging how they acted in a stress free environment. The questions that the interviewer asked were as follows:

Standard questions for young people

(1). How were you feeling before you started the Lightning Process?

(2). How did you come to choose the Lightning Process?

(3). Before starting the process, what were you expecting from it?

(4). What was the first session like for you?

(5). Tell me about later/further sessions?

(6). What aspects of the sessions did you think were helpful?

(7). What aspects of the sessions did you think were less helpful?

(8). Looking back, how do you feel about your experience of the Lightning Process

overall?

(9). How did the process compare with any other treatment you've had for CFS?

(10). Tell me about how you are feeling now?

(11). Looking back what are your thoughts about your illness?

(12). Is there anything else you want to tell me?

Standard questions for parents

(1). How were you and your child feeling before you started the Lightning Process?

(2). How did you come to choose the Lightning Process?

(3). Before starting the process, what were you expecting from it?

(4). What was the first session like for you?

(5). Tell me about later/further sessions?

(6). What aspects of the sessions did you think were helpful?

(7). What aspects of the sessions did you think were less helpful?

(8). Looking back, how do you feel about your experience of the Lightning Process

overall?

(9). How did the process compare with any other treatment your child had for CFS?

(10). Tell me about how your child is now?

(11). Looking back what are your thoughts about your child's illness?

(12). Is there anything else you want to tell me?

Reme et. al, 2012

Two out of the nine young people described the treatment as unhelpful, the rest mentioned that the treatment helped them on some level. These two tables show what the nine patients felt before and after the treatment. They were asked to describe their feelings both before and after with only one word.

Table i - Pre-treatment thoughts and expectations

1. *Positive*
2. *Positive*
3. *Few expectations*
4. *Nervous/anxious*
5. *Prepared to work hard*
6. *Mixed feelings about it*
7. *Influence from others*

37

8. *Positive*

9. *Negative*

Table ii - experiences with treatment

1. *Positive*

2. *Intensive*

3. *Confusing*

4. *Hard work*

5. *Conflicted with other treatments*

6. *General impression of effectiveness*

7. *Instant cure*

8. *Gradual improvement*

9. *Not helpful*

Reme et. al, 2012

Most of the patients considered the treatment to be potentially helpful before they started, so most of the young people went in with a willingness to at least try the techniques and open up to the interviewers. It is important to be open to these types of treatment as, similar to suggestion, treatment works on a basis of trust and conscious manipulation of the subconscious. This is blaringly obvious in patient number 9 who went in with a negative view of the treatment and considered it 'unhelpful' afterwards. Perhaps it is this method of 'thinking about thinking' that put some of the patients off the treatment as after the treatment, the results were varied. Some changed their opinion from positive to negative, others went from being impartial to saying that it helped them. As with any sort of treatment (especially psychological), there is a placebo effect. Some patients may have wanted the treatment to work, so they reviewed it as positive and in turn, it went on to cure them as other previous reported cases have shown to be possible. There is no hard and fast way to get rid of Chronic Fatigue as it revolves around a state of mind that is difficult to break away from without a change of lifestyle and attitude. But in general, we do well in things that we believe in, so that is really half the battle. Perhaps a better understanding of how we activate such dopaminergic pathways would help this theory as the only particularly useful tools that the Lighting Process offer are posture and movement. The focus of the study is on prevention of the acute stress response and the stress hormones that this psychological system produces and circulates. The cure is a variety of self-help techniques which can get very repetitive after a while, so a better choice of these would help patients immensely. To come up with more techniques, further research must be done into the Lighting Process as it is still very much in its infancy. But the more and more positive results from patients is a good sign that it is an alternative to pharmaceuticals for many young sufferers of this debilitating condition.

Exams

Exam procedure, the stress of achieving the best mark for the student and the exam technique preparation that the teacher has to drill into them, is not a pleasant time for most. It is only the highly organized who can structure their learning well enough in order to cover every topic well before the exam, the majority suffer long nights of Red Bull, cod liver oil and blueberries (most of the time spent researching is done not on the necessary subject matter but exploring Reddit for magic brain food). The last minute approach is condemned by many teachers because it doesn't actually get things to stick that well. But it does help in exams if you can cram everything in beforehand so it is fresh. The two serve different purposes and because of this, exams are usually not the time when your cognitive powers are at their peak.

The need for exam rituals outside of the classroom has been evident for a long time. There are always parents forcing their children to work every waking hour of the day so that they get the best out of them and give them the opportunities they will thank them for later. But sometimes it goes a little over the top. Take South Korea for example, now flourishing in the world of technology, it is economically independent and it has a very serious education system that is getting children to produce the best exam results in the world. The only trouble is, school doesn't seem to end for them. Their lives are completely focused on their education from the time they wake up at six in the morning to go to school, to four in the afternoon when they leave school, to seven in the evening when they go on to their after school programs, to ten at night when they go to a private tutor, to midnight or even later, when they are finally able to relax for a measly six hours before they get up and do it all over again. Contrast this with Finland's 3.5-hour day, and it makes you question how they both manage to achieve similar results in reading, writing and Maths tests. To some this may seem like an ideal situation for parents because their child is fulfilling her full potential. But when you consider that many parents in South Korea openly cheat in order to help their children compete in a world where exam results are everything, and that the country with a troubled past has the highest rate of teen suicide, it doesn't seem so glamourous. Henceforth, education researchers have been searching for some time to find a way to help students deal with the pressure of exams and get the best out of them in the process. There are many theories of how one can achieve this, as each person has his or her technique which was successful at one point or another. The problem is finding a set of general rules to follow that can structure one's learning and harness the full potential of the cognitive faculties. NLP research has had a go at this.

The model that one research study denotes, which provides a way of categorizing and organizing the underlying principles that should be followed when going into an exam, looks like this;

1. The student starts with a mental map of reality in its current format; however, this mental map is just that, a mental map, not reality.

2. Teacher practitioners of NLP apply various NLP principles that enhance dialogue between student and teacher.

3. The teacher shares specific NLP techniques (Techniques of Change) with students discussing strengths and weaknesses in the context of the student's personalized learning needs.

4. The student selects from a set of Techniques of Change noting that techniques do not need to be applied in their entirety in order to work. (Techniques of Change are robust to this sort of selection.)

5. Discussion and selection of Techniques of Change makes the construction of clearly defined goals (target setting processes) more meaningful to students.

6. Techniques of Change are then applied in a given learning situation.

7. The emerging experiences are interpreted in terms of feedback. (At this point it is essential to promote the

notion that there is no such thing as failure, only
feedback. This has a direct effect on the student.)

8. The student develops a new (more positive) mental map
of reality. The student acknowledges that their map can
be changed and as the map changes, behavior also
changes. This leads back to the starting point. The
student, appreciative of the benefits, can then re-enter the
cycle and negotiate the stages as frequently as they like
and within various educational contexts...

Kudliskis, 2009

This model was tested qualitatively on a group of thirty-six Psychology students in their final year at high school, before and after their A-Level exams. The 'exploratory action research study' lasted for over nine months (a whole school year). The aim of the study was to implement three aspects of NLP to the teaching methods used by their teachers and to find out the opinions of the students afterwards to see if they had made a difference or not. The three main areas of study were the underlying principles of NLP, an exploration of beliefs and goal setting, and an introduction to the strategies and 'Techniques of Change. All of which were deemed to be helpful in an exam situation. The particular questions and areas of focus that were applied to the study included; the exploration of and perceived value of clearly defined goals; the importance of the psychological interaction of the reticular activating system (RAS); the preference to operate within a comfort zone; the implementation and perceived values of 'Techniques of Change' such as affirmation, visualization and anchors; perception of inner barriers and outer barriers to success. The students' responses were varied but the extracts below are examples that seem to summarize best the general effect of NLP in the group of psychology students.

Jake - I think it's good to know what you are aiming for so you can think about steering towards it, as opposed to just going along and hoping you end up with good results.

Amy - Personally I think [the RAS] does really affect me and it does work. I am a very negative person and I do seem to see the negative side of things all the time and I don't necessarily process the positive. So I think [an awareness of the RAS] has had a major impact on my self-talk. I'm mainly negative towards myself and [the RAS] mainly filters the negative in and positive out. . . I guess I have always been negative [because] I've never wanted to build my hopes up. I have always thought aim low and then you are not going to be disappointed if you fail. I suppose I have always had that fear [of failure]. . . My attitude has slowly changed over the time as I have become more confident in myself and my abilities. It's taken a long time for me to become a bit more positive about myself.

Alison - [The powerful anchor] is my favorite one. At the moment this is really relevant to me, because I am panicking about my exams in January. [An anchor is] such a good thing when you are having a 'down moment' thinking "Oh God I'm going to fail!" Then, you remember how good it felt when you got [an 'A' in] the AS results, or, when I got my GCSEs. Everyone was happy. Then I think "Yes I can do this!" It gives you more motivation and you remember how you did it before and that you can do it again.

Rob - I think [visualization] is a good idea and I use it myself and I do quite a lot. It is almost like a form of revision in a way. . . If you visualize [the exam] and keep visualizing it, it becomes easier when you get into the exam. You won't have so much pressure on you. I know sports people use visualization on things like that to help them as it has good consequences.

Deeane - I used to turn round and say "I will do this". . . I wouldn't write it down but I would set myself a day on which I would do [it] and I would tell myself I would do [it]. . . This year I picked up retake Maths. . . I thought to myself [I will] do better because I have done it once. I know I can do better. . . and I think this term I have actually got better at it because I tell myself that I can do it better the second time round.

Sophie - [Negative expectations] hold me back, all the time, from what I could achieve. I know other people believe in me but I can't see that for myself some of the time. ... I think this is because when I was doing GCSEs, I was predicted much higher grades than I got and it kind of made me think I am not achieving what I could. But then I think maybe other people got it wrong, maybe I just can't achieve what they expect me to achieve. I think it was the same in AS, I expected much higher grades than I actually got and it just makes me think I can't do it. Maybe I'm not as intelligent as I thought and other people think.

Luke - My moods probably have a significant influence [on my learning]. . . [Sometimes] anger, maybe at myself, at not doing as much as I could have in preparation for the exam, or maybe if I have done very well then I will be happy. . .. [Emotions can sometimes act as] a spur to do better for the future. [However], I [often feel and] think I should do loads of work and then it sort of fades away.

Colette - [Stress] without a doubt [is an outer barrier to success]. If something is stressing me other than school, it inhibits my ability to focus on what I'm doing. . .. [Stress, for me, can be defined as] exam pressures, or [something in] a given [learning] situation that I want to resolve then and there, but it might not be appropriate to do so. But I can't let it go. If I can't deal with it, I can't do anything else at the time.

Deeanne - I feel that if I knew about NLP a lot earlier on I think it would have helped me a lot more. I think if I was told [about NLP] as soon as I started secondary school, I think I would have achieved a lot more, because I didn't have the affirmations and I didn't know how to talk to myself and tell myself how to do things, and I didn't know how to reframe. . .. I think nowadays with the amount of stress that young people go through NLP could be a way of [relieving that] stress and enhancing their education and achievement.

Amy - I did find [NLP] really interesting, it gave me loads of different techniques that I could use to change my personality, and my attitude. [NLP] has helped in a way as . . .. I have changed in myself and become the person who I like know. I really found the lessons enjoyable as well as useful.

Matty - I think [NLP] didn't just influence my learning in school, it really helped in other situations like for instance when I was learning to drive. [NLP] really helped me pass my test first time. Also, when playing tennis, I've become more positive . . . [I will] definitely continue to use [NLP]. Especially things like reframing.

Kudliskis, 2008

These extracts, as stated before, give a rounded picture of the overwhelmingly positive response from the students. There were very few negative comments, perhaps because the participants were all students of psychology, a related field to NLP and because of this the students associated their work to that of the NLP researchers'. But the responses seemed to be very precise, mentioning a particular technique of NLP that they liked and as such they appeared genuinely interested in the process and grateful for the opportunity to learn techniques that they could use to either help others or themselves. A lot of students reported on how NLP techniques such as RAS helped them overcome their negativity and anxiousness, a common condition when studying for exams. They also mentioned how exercising positive reinforcement helped them to focus when in the exam. It would appear, according to these results, that NLP helps in this capacity to suppress negative emotions and access positive ones. Negativity however is not so easily rooted out as it manifests in many ways that are difficult to spot with the naked eye. One may demonstrate a simple fear of failure, or the more complicated fear of success. The latter of which is more difficult to explain as it requires a deep understanding of oneself. It is often the cause of tense family relations that expect continual success or in some instances, a social group that expects the opposite. In any case, NLP was deemed able to relieve stress and negativity. Perhaps another way to do this could be the removal of negative anchors and replacing them with positive ones. For those who didn't suffer from negativity, techniques of NLP can be useful in improving focus by visualizing goals. Rob, one of the participants, mentioned that he was able to incorporate visualization into his revision, which is common amongst students of psychology based subjects of all levels as these revision methods are taught along with the target content in class. One particular technique that professors, lecturers and teachers use related to visualization is to imagine a safe place, usually a house or home, and fill each room with different subcategories of the main topic. Each subtopic should be represented with a visual aid so that the target content can be learnt through associating it with the object. This helps to disperse all of the information so that it is not clustered together and can be particularly helpful for spatio-visual learners. Other interviewees give a more general account of NLP, mentioning that it could be useful in the future for young, more impressionable learners and that it could be used outside of the classroom. There were various factors that need to be addressed though as the test did not assess the results of the students' exam grades after the nine months of NLP teaching against results of students who weren't taught these methods. The students were also all psychology students so would have considered the techniques useful for their topic as well as their technique. A controlled test aimed at younger students in a more common subject such as math or English may produce more usable results. But as a review of NLP, there are few students who could explain their experience and findings as well as psychology students, so for the type of experiment that Kudliskis carried out, the parameters of the test were suitable (Kudliskis, 2008).

Summary

Some would call for more testing to be done for NLP in education before generalizations can be made and teachers are trained with its specific, ambitious methods. Whilst a scientific explanation doesn't exist, and the theory is itself based on other psychological constructions which can't be proven, only gratified, NLP gives a solution to specific learning difficulties, albeit a rudimental one considering the limiting factors. It has received acclaim for helping communication in the classroom amongst those who struggle in that area. It has, for those who dedicated themselves to the model of NLP, improved their quality of life in education through the alleviation of stress, depression, fatigue and other debilitating conditions. NLP researchers make no claims that they have a better way for teachers to run their lessons, because there simply isn't enough evidence in areas that could prove or disprove the theory as a placebo. But as fMRI tests become increasingly available to the field of psycholinguistics, we are starting to see more and more telling factors, such as the positive effect of the reframing of a negative anchor on the amygdala. The methods may need refining, but the concept of NLP has been tested and revealed it to be a promising functional alternative to traditional teaching methods.

Chapter 3

Medical and Psychological Treatment

Although not a registered cure for any mental or physical illness, NLP has received attention from many in the field of medicine and psychiatric treatment as its numerous benefits have not gone unnoticed. The potential for NLP techniques to change the physiological wellbeing of patients has been mentioned in various studies testing the usability of such techniques as reframing anchors, replacing anchors, modelling behavior conducive to a healthy lifestyle, rapport building and emotional stability. In a medical crisis, the slightest hormonal change due to stress or other harmful stimuli could be fatal, so every effort is taken in order to lower cortisol levels. Of course these could be managed with drugs if the threat is imminent, but in non-lethal cases, it is preferable not to force it. That is why doctors, nurses and therapists undergo training courses in order to improve their bedside manner that helps them extract the most useful information out of calm patients which could save their lives. It not only helps to understand the situation better, it helps the relationship between patient and doctor and allows more natural conversation to happen in an environment where that is not an easy feat due to the presence of so many perceived potential harms leading to mental and physical barriers being erected. These barriers can be broken down, broken through or redesigned so that they don't cause problems any more, depending on the particular problem.

In situations where a condition is not immediately dangerous but could be through diachronic change, NLP is claimed to be most effective as the process requires time for the body to heal itself. It is not likely that NLP will save someone's life when excessive damage has been done, but it could give them a better chance. Incidentally, the word 'but' is a trigger word that NLP researchers consider dangerous and advise that it should be used sparingly. This is because it can change a patient's state of mind instantaneously from good to bad, bad to worse or from bad to good but in each case, the sudden fluctuation can lead patients to feel nauseous with all of the contradictory signals that the body is sending, causing internal chaos. There have been reports that claim that an excessively enthusiastic or happy state can lead us to disease as well as a depressed state, so the chemicals need to be regulated. Another trigger word that is thought to lead to a negative, and sometimes dangerous internal response is 'try'. If for example, a doctor was to say, "We will try to remove all of the cancer," a patient will go in worrying that not all will be removed, encouraging an emergency response which could put the patient at greater risk before going into surgery. On the other hand, if a doctor said, "We will see if we can remove all of the cancer," the implications are slightly different. With the use of the word 'try', the doctor is insinuating that it is a complex operation which needs to be done and that it would be risky to say that it will work and make the patient better. In the latter example, the insinuation is that it is one of many operations that can be done in an effort to eventually rid the patient of cancer. In the former, the patient is given the impression that it is do or die time, the ultimatum is implicated as the doctor has stated that his intentions are to terminate the problem there and then. The latter implicates an exploratory mission to 'see' what can be done and then move on from there. These phrases, as you can imagine, are echoed in the phonological loop of the patient's mind, so it is important that doctors and nurses choose their words carefully. If not, the patient could be thinking more about 'the end' as opposed to getting better, which sends the body the wrong message at a critical time. Similarly, it is important that a patient believes a doctor when she says, "don't worry" because if not, patients can become conflicted, confused and possibly either angry or scared at the prospects because their instincts are telling them that they are not going to make it as the doctor's body language projects uncertainty. This, according to NLP advocates, can be remedied with 'soft eyes' and other relaxation techniques that help to put the doctor or nurse at ease and in turn, the patient. 'Soft eyes' refers to a form of focusing vision on a person or object whilst simultaneously being aware of one's surroundings using one's peripheral vision. It appears to be more natural in conversation and, as the name suggests, less intensive.

These techniques, be they linguistic or behavioral, are not just used by doctors, therapists and nurses in treatment. They can be used by the patients themselves if they believe in them and take them seriously. As with any such psychological treatment, there is the placebo effect which leads to irregularities in results, but generally speaking if someone trusts in something they will make it work for themselves. At least, they won't admit they invested themselves in a lie lightly. This is often the driving force with such treatments as there aren't the resources to diagnose exactly which psychological treatment, be it CBT, NLP or hypnotherapy to use in which circumstance. So patients need to trust and invest themselves in the treatment to give it hope to succeed. It is said that only the weak minded may be hypnotized, which may be true on some level as according to hypnotherapists, one must be open to change and trust in the hypnotist if he is to be treated in this manner. The treatment wouldn't exist in this capacity if there was no weakness, so it is safe to say that if the patient was weak beforehand, he could come out stronger after it. Understanding and acting upon attenuating symptoms should be something that patients do in their own time, so say doctors such as Matt James who has long revered the benefits of working with such models as NLP.

Phobias

One of the most prevalent mental health problems today is phobias. They can range from the common, more treatable phobias such as claustrophobia to ablutophobia (fear of cleaning oneself) which is more difficult to treat as there are few reported cases of it and the anchor which is causing the problem is more difficult to uncover. Phobias can be categorized into three hypernymic categories. 'Specific phobias' includes five sub-categories, a fear of animals, a fear of the natural environment, situational fear, blood-injection-injury phobia and other; 'social phobia' which can be subdivided into the hyponyms generalized social phobia and specific social phobia (the latter is situational); 'agoraphobia' which is the fear and anxiety of crowded spaces. The cause of a phobia is known as an anchor. It creates the phobia by creating an association (usually unconscious) between a stimulus (the anchor) and an emergency response. Anchors can be kinaesthetic, auditory, visual, or a combination of the three depending on the memory. For instance, a certain song could be the cause of an unnatural fear of new things (neophobia) because it reminds the sufferer of a particular time when he tried something new and it had disastrous consequences. This particular phobia is common amongst the elderly because they are more 'set in their ways' than younger people, implying that they have a stronger sense of identity. It can be disheartening for older people to fail at something that is popular amongst younger people but which is new and challenging to them. Because of this, anchors such as songs, places or feelings are unconsciously put in place as a barrier or mental block in order to maintain the memory or phobia of that instance to avoid perceived future embarrassment. It is more often however that the root cause and subsequent anchoring process happened at a very young age, as there are many who have suffered from a phobia their whole life and who are afraid to confront it because of a repressed fear of how it could affect them. These instances are harder to treat as to recollect a moment that happened at a very young age is difficult due to children's inconsideration of potentially pertinent factors.

The collapsing of the anchor not only requires that the anchor is uncovered and dealt with, it requires another stronger anchor to replace it, reframing of the anchor or the more traditional approach which is to accustom the patient to the associative meaning of the anchor so that they accept it. Replacing and reframing anchors are NLP methods and are also thought to be the most functional and successful. In order to replace an anchor, the new anchor needs to be stronger and more resilient than the last, so a psychologist will have to deliberate whether a potential new anchor serves the purpose of being more positive than the previous one is negative. The negative anchor must also be removed before the positive one replaces it or else the former could compete with it and revive itself, often manifesting in another guise. One way that therapists do this is to locate both the phobia and the desirable state of mind, then address the patient and get him to recall firstly the positive state and then the negative state in turn whilst associating each with a different object. The two would then be imagined together, the negative one would be disassociated first leaving the positive anchor as the surviving association of the memory. For example, a patient could have a fear of the sea because of a time when she nearly drowned. She feels the same way whenever she sees the sea, in a negative light, but she enjoys the beach as most of us do. So the fact that she enjoys the beach can be used as the positive anchor to replace the negative, but first it needs conditioning so that it is a more powerful driving force than the negative anchor. This can be achieved with relative ease once more is known about the patient. The psychologist may use anchor the association of the sea and freedom for instance, enticing the patient to feel that instead of killing her, the sea will free her. The patient is asked to imagine how free she may feel swimming in the ocean and soon after, asked to think of the phobic response that has crippled her for her whole life. The patient is then told to stop imagining the phobic response and continue imagining herself swimming freely in the sea. At this point, the phobic anchor should have been replaced with the positive one.

Reframing an anchor is a similar concept to replacing it, only the technique differs. Some phobias are stronger than others, and such trauma as PTSD (post-traumatic stress disorder) is immune to replacement therapy as just thinking about an incident can cause very high stress levels, so they need a different approach. Reframing the troubling anchor is actually easier than replacing it all together, as it is only 'shedding some light' on it or giving the anchor a 'silver lining', or however you want to look at it. Let's take the same example of a patient who has a phobia of the sea and who is using a negative anchor to rule her way of thinking. Reframing the anchor means maintaining the negative anchor, and turning it into a positive one. So the same concept of drowning is referred to, but instead of the patient focusing on the fact that she nearly drowned and lost her life, the focus would be on how she managed to get out of that situation, making her a survivor who could overcome the elements. The fear that once ruled her evolves into strength as it can be drawn on in a situation when it is needed. This treatment has been known to work temporarily but it is also common for the patient to regress into doubt and the phobia returns soon after.

One study aimed to test the use of NLP in treating phobias by using a hybrid model of the two techniques and also draws on areas of traditional psychology such as exposure therapy. One of the key principals of the V/KD phobia cure as it's known, is to make the patient feel that they are not being singled out, and that bad things happen to everyone. So just talking about similar issues and looking at problems from a third person perspective helps. This method of dissociation is applied through a sort of role play that sees the therapist and the patient in a cinema where the context revolves around the patient watching a movie of their life. Firstly, a kinaesthetic 'safety anchor' is put in place, a time when the patient felt safe. This is made, maintained and strengthened in the process by holding hands with the therapist. The patient is then asked to imagine watching a movie of himself up to the point in time before their phobia took hold and before the negative experience happened. The patient is then asked to imagine himself 'floating out' of his body to observe himself watching the movie of himself, creating a double disassociated state that leads to emotional distance from the events leading up to the phobia. This is a powerful tool of NLP as the patient is not focusing on the events leading up to the start of the phobia, he is visualizing the effect that it has on another version of him whilst another different version of himself is reliving it. The treatment continues with the therapist asking the patient to change the sub-modalities of the picture in disturbing parts of the film to make the image smaller or darker in order to decrease its latency. The film is replayed until all of the negative events leading up to the start of the phobia are diminished. The movie is then replayed, in full color at the end to black and white at the beginning at a fast speed to obscure where the changes were made. This can be repeated until the memory is neutralized. It has been successful on many patients with varying degrees of phobias, some who have spent thousands on unsuccessful therapies, but none whom suffer from PTSD or other serious afflictions (Bandler and Grinder, 1979).

Whilst there is some skepticism about the reliability of NLP techniques in relieving people of phobias, there are few reported cases that state that there were no positive effects of the treatment. The most common argument against the model in therapy is that the conscious mind is can be resistant to change when it knows that it is being targeted, and as the techniques require the conscious mind to be in a pliable state, the therapy can be inconsistent as not everyone is open to techniques of therapy. But one of the principals of all of the NLP phobia treatments is trust, built through an anchor or through physical, kinaesthetic contact. There is also the notion that most of those who suffer from a phobic condition want to get better. There is then a strong motive for patients to succeed and because of this, they are more frequently than not, open to follow the instructions of therapists.

Post Stroke

There is no known psychological treatment for victims who have suffered an Ischemic stroke. Usually in stroke cases, a patient will be made aware of the dangers, and told that they will never be the same again. That they will never be independent because it is too dangerous, that they will struggle with everyday activities and in serious cases they are told that they may not live much longer. This leads to extreme depression and anxiety in about 60% of patients who have been treated for ischemic stroke of varying degrees. Depression and anxiety are two of the most common conditions that stroke patients endure after they have been to hospital, and surprisingly this is generally ignored after a patient has been discharged, left up to the family of the victims to muddle together whatever helpful information they can find on the internet. There are of course many support groups for stroke victims worldwide, but no information of techniques that survivors can use in order to make their lives more pleasant or at least more bearable after a stroke. It is important that stroke victims are given continuous care because there have been countless reported cases of panic attacks and crippling loneliness due to anxiety and depression, which can be seriously dangerous for their well-being in such a fragile state. Just an elevated heart rate could cause a patient to panic and subsequently, stress them out to a point where they are damaging themselves in an important recovery period and making their prognosis worse. An alarming amount of stroke survivors are still crippled by anxiety and depression five years after the event, some 30% of them. Drugs can be prescribed for such situations but there have been documented cases of them harming patients and others that state that its effects are so short-term that they cannot be maintained. There is another matter of the damaged neural pathways associated with emotion regulation, which may never recover, leaving stroke patients without their natural resources to combat negative emotions such as depression and anxiety. It is therefore perhaps ambitious to say that a psychological treatment could do any real, lasting good for stroke patients after their initial physiological treatment. And efforts in the past have not yielded any notable findings. But a recent study has found a combination of NLP techniques and health education to be a success for many patients immediately after they had been discharged.

This study was established on the grounds of Bandler and Grinder's research into NLP phobias as well as the use of NLP in treating breast cancer and external cephalic vision that others came up with. As the main purpose of the study was to help reduce stress and panic attacks in stroke patients, the methods for achieving this that were selected for the procedure were all easy to master, relaxation techniques. They include, but are not limited to; breathing skill to increase strength; negative thought conversation skill; pressure-reducing method; coordination training method to control heart rate; and meditation to quieten the mind. They were then explained in detail, over the course of 4 days, how to use these techniques and were all educated in health studies focusing on ischemic stroke. The results were assessed six months after the patient was discharged so that the researchers could check-up and see if the patients still showed signs of depression and anxiety. Table 1 shows the details of the patients before the test began.

Table 1. Baseline characteristics of patients

Characteristic	Intervention group (n = 90)	Control group (n = 90)
Age (mean ± SD, y)	60.3 + 9.9	59.7 + 10.5
Male (n, %)	63 (70.0)	67 (74.4)
Married (n, %)	87 (96.7)	88 (97.8)
Educational level (n, %)		
Elementary	51 (56.7)	55 (61.1)
High school	23 (25.6)	25 (27.8)
College or university	16 (17.8)	10 (11.1)
Occupation (n, %)		
Office worker	16 (17.8)	8 (8.9)
Laborer	19 (21.1)	27 (30.0)
Retired	45 (50.0)	39 (43.3)

Unspecified	10 (11.1)
16 (17.8)	
Income per month (n, %)	
Less than 1000 RMB	18 (20.0)
28 (31.1)	
1,000-3000 RMB	57 (63.3)
53 (58.9)	
More than 3000 RMB	15 (16.7)
9 (10.0)	
Medical comorbidity (n, %)	
Hypertension	70 (77.8)
64 (71.1)	
Diabetes mellitus	19 (21.1)
16 (17.8)	
Coronary artery disease	12 (13.3)
16 (17.8)	
Hyperlipidemia	24 (26.7)
24 (26.7)	
BMI (mean 6 SD)	24.3 + 3.2
24.1 + 3.0	
Current smoking (n, %)	35 (38.9)
37 (41.1)	

Current alcohol dependence (n, %)	6 (6.7)	5 (5.6)
History of stroke (n, %)	22 (24.4)	25 (27.8)
Duration between stroke and hospitalization (M[P25-P75])	3 (1-11)	3 (1-6)
Length of hospital stay	11.5 + 3.54	11.54 + 4.78
Location of lesions (n, %)*		
Left hemisphere	41 (46.1)	38 (42.7)
Right hemisphere	34 (38.2)	43 (48.3)
Left and right hemisphere	10 (11.2)	6 (6.7)
Other locations	4 (4.5)	2 (2.2)
Severity of stroke		
Mild	67 (74.4)	57 (63.3)
Moderate	20 (22.2)	30 (33.3)

Severe   3 (3.3)
3 (3.3)

Abbreviation: BMI, body mass index; SD, standard deviation.
*Data are missing for 2 participants (intervention n 5 1, control n 5 1) in this item.

Peng et. al, 2015

Table 2 shows the number of patients who suffered from depression and anxiety at different points in the treatment.

Table 2. Proportion of patients with depression and anxiety between groups at different time points

	Depression		Anxiety	
Time Point	Intervention n (%)	Control n (%)	Intervention n (%)	Control n (%)

73

Baseline	52 (57.8)	53 (58.9)
55 (61.1)	45 (50.0)	
After intervention	16 (17.8)	34 (37.8)
21 (23.3)	36 (40.0)	
Six-month follow-up	5 (6.3)	8 (10.5)
4 (5.1)	10 (13.2)	

Peng et.al, 2015

The key findings here are that immediately after the intervention of NLP and health education, there is a huge difference between the number of patients who received it and those who didn't. Only sixteen patients felt the effects of depression immediately after the intervention compared to the thirty-four who weren't treated. Another prominent finding, although slightly obscured by the unevenness of the baseline results, was that 40% of the patients who were taught about NLP and health education claimed to have had their anxiety cured after the intervention whilst only 10% of the control group (nine patients) exhibited signs of reduced anxiety after they had been at the hospital for three weeks (the same time the results of intervention group were assessed after four days of therapy over three weeks). Whilst there was little difference in the results at the six month follow up for depression, there were only four patients out of the original fifty-five in the intervened group who showed signs of anxiety at that point of the study, and ten out of the original forty-five in the control group who showed signs having not had the luxury of an intervention.

The results tell us that a little understanding can go a long way when patients suffer from depression or anxiety post stroke. Even if it is just letting patients know that they are not alone and that the emotions they are feeling are common and manageable is comforting. So often is the case, particularly with young people, that after a stroke happens people give up hope of ever living a normal, happy life. This is partly due to the public perceptions of stroke victims, and the ignorance surrounding it. The common perception is that strokes only happen to old people, which simply isn't true, but worse than that, to some people stroke victims can seem 'weak', 'retarded' or 'intoxicated'. These perceptions come from a complete lack of understanding of what a victim has suffered. Maybe people think that they were born like this, making that somehow more acceptable to lance toxic pernicious jeers at other people. Teenagers such as Sarah Scott who suffered from ischemic stroke are constantly subjected to abuse. People say that she is 'drunk', or 'smoking something' or 'stupid'. She has had to overcome her condition, which can frequently lead to anxiety and depression, in spite of such negativity slung towards her. Sarah's aphasia affected Broca's area in the brain and subsequently, her ability to comprehend complex grammatical expressions and use sometimes simple words and phrases. Her intellect remained however unaffected and she now works as a science technician in a school. Not too shabby for a girl who was once almost paralyzed and who is still in recovery from a crippling disease that we would rather not imagine. It would be helpful then, if we all improved our awareness of stroke symptoms and considered ways of helping those who suffer from this horrid condition.

There were few limitations in the study testing the usability of NLP techniques and health education for stroke victims, leading the results to appear even more exciting. The only limiting factors that could have affected the results were the lack of quality control, the patients talking between themselves, the placebo effect and the different baseline characteristics of patients. But these factors are thwarted by the crevasse of difference between the control group and the intervention group. It is highly likely that the techniques and information that the intervention group were given helped a lot. And after only four brief sessions over three weeks.

Determining the most important techniques out of those that were studied, and future methodologies, will require a separate qualitative evaluation. Another study for instance based on the verbal feedback patients, rather than their score on the HAM-D (Hamilton Depression Test) and the HAM-A (Hamilton Anxiety Test) which requires very selective data may be a good alternative. This could demonstrate the usability of each technique individually which was only very briefly described in this test. The initial research that Peng did explained the potential, untested intervention method that was based on other mental models and constructs.

"...successful psychotherapy can produce a positive influence on mental illness, neurotransmitters,

neurotrophic factors, stress hormones, and immune factors and regulate neurobiochemical function and neuroendocrine– immunity system. These can facilitate nerve conduction, relieve stress reaction, and regulate immune function and finally improve physical function of patients. The intervention consists of many NLP techniques: breathing skill to relax and increase strength, negative thought conversion skill, pressure-reducing method, coordination training method to control the heart rate, and meditation to increase mental energy. The means by which the entire course produces a positive effect was not directly determined in this study. One possible explanation is that the interventionists helped patients to shift negative thoughts or beliefs to more positive ones and learn how to release pressure and relax in hospitalization and in future. In addition, health education had promising effects on the health beliefs to patients. A better psychological status and a healthier lifestyle may be the reason of improvement..."

Peng et. al, 2015

These methods are not difficult to master. They are also not difficult to teach as a clinician with only a rudimental knowledge of NLP was in charge of making the patients and their families aware of NLP techniques and health education. With such a common disease like ischemic stroke, having no psychological cure for that which affects one's psychology leaves room for a lot of work to be done. Medics may focus on the physiological aspects, and so they should, but for stroke victims, the condition extends to day-to-day life outside of the hospital. They need a way to use their natural responses such as fear to let them know when something is wrong and control any irregularities such as hormone imbalance that most post stroke patients endure. They can also be made aware of such positive factors as, even after a stroke, full cognitive function of the brain can be restored by simply diverting traffic on neuron pathways around the dead grey matter of the brain. This can also help victims of aphasic damage to Broca's area as their search and retrieval faculties can be practiced using NLP techniques. As with many things, visualizing the problem helps a lot. With this technique, imagine a blocked road, neural highway. Due to a massive lump of dead grey matter in the middle of the road that is forcing traffic to a halt, you have to find another way around to get to your destination. This means travelling through lots of narrow B-roads, but your destination is always going to be there. This understanding, that you don't actually lose anything of real value that you can't find again after a stroke, could be the difference between a complete recovery and a partial one.

Addiction

Addiction is so common that just about everyone would admit to having a frequent itch that needs to be scratched. It could be something as harmless as chocolate (in moderation) but sometimes it rears its ugly head in the form of toxic substance abuse. Alcohol and tobacco are the most common of these toxic substances to be overindulged in and as such they are the focus of many psychological studies that aim to put an end to these nasty habits. There are a number of explanations as to why some people are more prone to addiction than others. One common psychological theory is that, in the case of smoking, a cigarette can act as a kind of pacifier, which is indicative of abandonment as in this case a person is replaced with a cigarette. It is also sometimes referred to in psychology as a fake friend, because it also helps people with intimacy issues get 'close' to something other than themselves. It has been known to be helpful in times of loss too, because again it provides a certain attachment which acts as a substitute for a lost person or thing. In all of these cases, and many others, the cause isn't so much due to the gratifying physical effects that alcohol or tobacco provide, it's down to the individual having something to depend upon. Especially with tobacco, because the effects aren't all that noticeable after one has built up a tolerance, as people with addictions tend to do after a period of time. It is an easy way to mark certain emotive states and important times in one's life. To have that positive and negative reinforcement is necessary for some as without regulation of their actions and feelings, they can't move past them. There is also the reward system which it provides us with; having a drag or a drink after completing an action, however small it may be, gives us that pat on the back that we need to, again, move forward. And this is why it is so difficult to stop, because everybody knows that you have to do an emergency stop after you've been going too fast for your own good. And it can be a painful experience if not done under the right conditions. It might also come back to bite us if we don't exercise restraint because it is so easy to get back behind the wheel if the petrol station is open 24 hours, it's two miles down the road and it has that reward that we earnt for quitting for a (rather longer than usual) couple of weeks. Very few of us give up on the first try. I would go as far as to say that it would be unlikely to stick if you did. Quitting something like smoking and regulating something like alcohol requires low points to show us just how dependent we are on these substances and how detrimental it could be to put a harmful and addictive substance in charge of regulating our emotional state and well-being. So from a non-pharmacological point of view, addiction is largely psychological. Of course, the pills, patches, inhalers, non-alcoholic beer, other pills, whatever, may make a difference, but they won't sort out the underlying cause of addiction. NLP has had some success in dealing with the root cause of addiction as its techniques such as cognitive-perceptual reconstruction target the way addictions take hold of people.

One influential pioneer of NLP techniques, Tom Hoobyar, has said in his book 'The Essential Guide to Neuro Linguistic Programming' that he originally became an NLP user after he used one of its techniques to give up smoking tobacco after thirty-six years of being addicted, eighteen of which he was trying to give it up (Hoobyar, T and Dotz, T et. al 2013). That is quite a struggle, and one which evidently has converted the boss of a successful start-up firm to a NLP practitioner and teacher. Another more detailed study of the effects of NLP on the addiction to smoking was done by Dr. Miguel Enriquez. He concluded, after testing conventional treatment methods in two control groups of ten participants in each, and NLP treatment methods in one other group of ten participants, that the NLP techniques were by far the most successful of the three techniques. In studies of alcoholism, researchers have found similarly positive results. A review done by Laurence Miller integrates, "brain-behavioral perspectives with the data on personality and psychopathology, focusing on the relevance of a multidimensional neuropsychological model to psychodynamic concepts of ego functioning and the substance abusers' problems in the regulation of affect and behavior" (1990). It is argued that the concept of cognitive style is useful for understanding the relationship of neuropsychological functioning to personality dynamics, and that this approach can be especially useful in the understanding and treatment of addictions. Miller claims that most alcoholics suffer from impulsive character disorder or low ego strength. Other factors to be considered are field dependency, external locus of control, attenuated time extension and disturbed object relations which lead to problems such as abstract concept formation, set-maintenance, set-shifting, behavioral control, and cognitive flexibility. So there are plenty of reasons to look into treating a disorder such as alcoholism which could have manifested into a much more difficult to treat condition that can define aspects of one's personality. Some researchers have gone as far as to compile their research on this topic to make a book that encompasses relevant thoughts on how to treat alcoholism. They include ideas including cognitive-perceptual reconstruction, hypnotic communication, and rapport skills for therapists, sorting mechanisms in the basic human programs and co-dependency. I have just mentioned a lot of terms and conditions, so I will try in the next paragraph to explain, without so many commas and so much jargon, how they gel together to form a better understanding of addiction.

We so frequently feel unpleasant things as a result of our brain telling our body that something is wrong even when we don't know exactly what the problem is. Sometimes the problem just isn't that obvious, other times the problem is so contrived and implausible that we don't believe it when we think of it so we look for another problem. Sometimes our brain tricks us into thinking that there is a problem when there isn't, in an effort to make things easier for itself. But sometimes the brain is inconsiderate and doesn't look after the body. Take this case for example; when Dianne broke up with Tom, she got stomach cramps. The doctors could find no physiological reason for the cramps, so she went to see a psychiatrist. The psychiatrist uncovered a hidden memory from Dianne's childhood, from when her mother left her, of her pretending that she had stomach cramps in a bid to get her mother to stay. This memory commanding a bodily response had been lying dormant and caused Dianne to feel that she wanted Tom to stay, but according to her psychiatrist it was more likely that her abandonment issues had surfaced and influenced the emergency response rather than her willingness to let Tom back into her life. This is an example of how the unconscious mind uses the body to trick the conscious mind into doing something it doesn't want to do. Contrary to the old 'follow your heart' or 'follow your gut' mottos, the non-existent 'follow your subconscious' saying could be covertly misleading. This, incidentally, was the reason why Tom Hoobyar (not Dianne's Tom) succumbed to his craving after his father died. On the way to his father's house he caved and stopped to buy cigarettes because his subconscious mind tricked his conscious mind into feeling that it was ok to smoke at a stressful time such as this, when it would probably make it worse and make him more susceptible to stressful stimuli in the future. It is only in understanding our actions, from a conscious and unconscious perspective that we can help ourselves overcome addiction and stop abstract concepts forming, telling us that we should systematically follow certain compulsive behaviors. 'Cognitive-Perceptual Reconstruction' is one way patients can overcome addiction. By using techniques that bring together the inner child and the adult through re-anchoring, re-imprinting and even olfactory (sense of smell) techniques amongst others, the patient uses his conscious mind to search for and negotiate a compromise with internally conflicting parts, bringing together the past and present versions of his self. Other such Meta models incorporate the locus of family ties. Some people have siblings who can act as 'scape goats' or distractions for them. So their addiction will go unnoticed due to the focus on the other sibling who demonstrates more obvious signs of addiction. There is also the problem of 'co-dependency' in many addicts. This refers to the tendency for one to break rules and it is usually demonstrated in children who have been given lots of rules at home or at school. There are many reasons why people become addicted to substances and why they exhibit self-detrimental behavior after or during the giving-up saga. Some say it's boredom, others have underlying problems they feel like they are addressing. Any which way you look at it, addiction is not healthy behavior. In Tom's case, hypnotherapy didn't work in the long run. That isn't to say that it won't work for everyone because there are lots of documented cases reporting its effectiveness, just none that follow up after a year to see if the patient is still smoking or drinking. This could be because the patients don't have techniques to help themselves when the hypnotherapist isn't around. Or it could be because hypnotherapy is the art of tricking patients into thinking that they are cured, preying on their lack of knowledge of the mind and using that to plant ideas. NLP does just the opposite. It tricks you, and then reveals how it tricked you. So you aren't left wondering where the rabbit in the hat came from (Hoobyar, T and Dotz, T et. al 2013).

Summary

Treatment is one of the first places where researchers of new mental models aim their research towards. It is the one place where it can help the most, aiding those who are in sometimes desperate need of help. There are millions of people willing to try new prosperous techniques and procedures, some people will even try new pharmacological treatment because they are out of options, so psychological treatments should be encouraged in hospitals seeing as they can do no physical harm and the psychological benefits can be very helpful indeed. Equally, they can be useful outside of treatment for people who have suffered from illnesses that affect the mind, especially aphasia, phobias, addiction, depression and anxiety which have seen positive results. NLP techniques can be very simple to learn and as various studies have shown, well worth the minimal amount of effort needed to re-imprint, reframe, replace, reinvent memories and feelings that can be dangerous to one's health in the long term. Seeing a psychiatrist may cost too much, hypnotherapy may be too unreliable, pharmaceuticals may cause more problems than positives, friendly advice may not be enough to deal with exasperating, perplexing molestations. But NLP is a readily available alternative to the imperfect psychological aid options for patients in and out of treatment.

Chapter 4

Business

Sales representatives, advertisers, public relation officers and business executives, have been accused of using persuasive techniques such as NLP to sell their business, so people actively look out for them when they see a billboard or slicked back hair attached to a three-piece suit. They have to keep getting smarter about how they market products and sell the public on buying them. PR is a field in which little comments in articles framing a product in a positive light can go unnoticed by the conscious mind, but may hold trigger words that trick the unconscious into buying a product. And as such it has become a popular medium for companies to sell themselves and their products. The advertising system is considered to be an annoying but necessary industry by many. It is reliant on huge sums of money rather the quality of the product or the idea itself, because it is generally Quantitative not qualitative. If the system was in place for the benefit of consumers, there would be government issued corporations not NGO's in control of adverts that employed research teams to assess products' value and only show unbiased reviews. Unbiased reviews do exist (at least we think they do), but you have to look for them, because they don't have the immense funding that monopolies and oligopolies have. Consider the latest Bond film 'Spectre' for example. The bond franchise is one of the most famous brands in history and as such, it was a big catch for Heineken, who used Bond's image at just about every opportunity in their product placement. They payed obscene money to be able to do this. But not only this, they can also sue people for using their name in a negative way due to the massive amount they shelled out for intellectual property rights. Similarly, Coca-Cola can sue for using the 'Coca-Cola Red' which they have trademarked. There is some debate as to how far corruption can reach after such scandals as the bribing of FIFA president Step Blatter, it seems like money can influence big decisions or even buy power. It certainly has been the case with Republican candidate Donald Trump, who wouldn't have been able to fund his campaign without millions of his billions of dollars (which he can get back if he wins the vote anyway). The problem is that we only hear about the things that these brands like Heineken, Coca-Cola and Trump want us to hear about.

They may include negative elements of the product to get the consumer to believe that they are receiving an unbiased review of the product, inspiring trust in the company and product. But nobody is going to pay millions to get their name in the public eye and then give a list of all of the pros and cons of that product. They are going to sell it with a technique that best suits a particular product and situation. It could mean building rapport with a client or a consumer, it could mean making them laugh, it could mean assuring them that potential problems are necessary, it could require a combination of all three.

Advertising

In the hectic world of advertising, companies employ people with a certain skillset. A professional in advertising should be able to hone in on public opinion and consumer mentality to offer or package a product in a way that will convince as many people as possible that they need it. This can be done a number of different ways. The traditional way to market a product is to focus the advert towards it, highlighting all the positives and making little or no reference to parts of the product that could damage its reputation. But something as simple as a one-sided message gets old very quick. It is very boring for viewers, listeners or readers to have to follow an explanatory procedure that explains in a lot of detail, why you need this product. If every advert was like that, just about everyone watching or listening would tune out in advert breaks and the millions spent on air time would be wasted. That isn't to say that this method isn't still used to some effect today by advertising companies, but it is used sparingly in most cases. Charities and law firms employ this approach because they delineate presuppositions of serious ideals that may lose integrity if a joke is used to make a product more pleasurable to watch or incongruous statements are made for the audience to resolve. The purpose for such adverts as these is to portray the product as a necessity rather than a luxury and as such, they require a very sincere tone. But most products that are advertised have multiple purposes, and most of them are not wholly dependent on an audience requiring the subject of the advertisement to maintain their socioeconomic status or survive due to the Western world's efficiency at accommodating these factors. Most capitalist countries advertise items that 'should' be had or 'could' be had, directed at a certain demographic. One common advertising technique to glamourize a product of this nature is to add humor and sex, sometimes together as they are often intrinsically linked, sometimes separately. Humor especially, creates positive associations with a brand or product, and has been proven to be a successful way to market almost anything time and time again. One problem with using humor in advertising is that it can portray a product as a joke, and therefore should not be used for something serious such as a foundation for incurable diseases. Source credibility is often also damaged because a joke may not be perceived as funny by everyone and if the humor is lost on the audience, they will create negative connotations associated with the product. Similarly, if an advert is to be repeated and people are prone to experience it more than once, humor can lose its ability to entice people into investing in something. There is also the context to consider; if for example the concept of death as a joke is used in a situation where sensitivity is necessary due to the possibility of people dying whilst using the advertised product or a similar product (a car for instance) then the advert will have brought up negative associations in the mind of the consumer, putting them off the product in turn. It may seem like a good idea for someone who has never experienced a car crash but for a large majority, it causes a conscious or unconscious mistrust of the product. For those products that already have a bad reputation, a memorable and positive reformation of a brand item or the brand itself can be achieved by mentioning a commonly known problem and combatting it with a positive aspect. Similar to the positive anchor replacement technique in treatment, this positive aspect needs to be more pertinent than the negative aspect for this to be a success, and more often than not, this will vary in public opinion. In cases such as these though, when a brand is in need of reformation due to previous issues with image, the positives outweigh the negatives if the advert is done correctly. These types of adverts don't allow for the same novelty value that humor provides and the subsequent attentiveness of the audience, but it does give the product and the brand credibility which is a necessity for situations when a product has initially failed or if a brand is in its infancy. Both situations require the company to broaden its long standing client base and this is best achieved through reputation and credibility in the field (Mann, S et. al. 2012).

The three techniques mentioned above are three of the most common ways advertisers promote their product. One-sided messages, humor and two-sided messages have been used for decades and have been a cornerstone in the rise of capitalism. They are however being gradually sussed out by the public and unless the advert does enough to distract the audience from its persuasive intent, the advert will likely be seen as untrustworthy. The NLP technique of reframing has been used in various contexts where people have had to break potentially negative news or feedback in a way that diminishes the negative aspects and puts more weight on the positive. It is similar to the two-sided message when applied to advertising in that it implies a positive image that is stronger than the negative precursor that it also denotes. The difference is that the reframing technique does not give both a good and bad point like the two-sided message does, it gives one point which is publicly known to be negative, and it puts a positive spin on it. When selling a new energy drink with image problems such as the use of taurine, a two-sided message approach would mention a possible negative side effect of taurine such as, "taurine may cause psoriasis," and then give apropos positive mention to the fact that, "taurine is crucial to a number of physiological processes." When reframing in this situation on the other hand, one would refer to the negative and color it as positive, so the combined message may read, "our scientists are loaded with taurine and they work fifteen hours a day to crack safe, consumable energy." In this example, no negative aspect is mentioned, it is implied and the audience is invited to infer the negative implication from their previous knowledge of the product and chemical. There are the positive implications that taurine helps the scientists making the drink more focused and that they are researching 'safe' alternatives. Taurine is therefore portrayed as a low risk substance that is used by smart people and it hints that it can lead to improvements in well-being. This is of course a hypothetical situation, but it has been used in high status companies such as Mercedes Benz. They had a problem with the image of their A-Class as it failed the Elk test so rather than employing the two-sided method in an advert to outright state the problem and win back the trust of their long standing client base, they went for a more novel approach that focused more on the product than the brand image. Mercedes reframed the failed Elk test as a valuable learning experience with the insinuation that they learn more from their mistakes than their successes. They achieved this through Boris Becker saying that, "I learned more from my throw-backs than I did from my successes." The negative associations that came with failing the Elk test had become the same reason why the A-Class overcame its faults and made it noticeably better. Granted, this technique requires the audience to know previous knowledge relating to the failed test so this advert may only be usable at a specialized event like a car show room. It also requires the audience to have some knowledge and respect for the reputation that Mercedes have crafted over the years which allow them to use irony and incongruity instead of finding a way to gain back the trust of their client base. It should also be noted that the friendly face of Boris Becker probably played its part as well in gaining back the trust of the clientele. So the reframing method in advertising can be effective in certain situations but they require two important factors, trust and exposure to be successful (Neudecker, N and Esch, F, et. al. 2014).

The reframing method was tested in advertising in a study led by Niels Neudecker, a German psychologist who wanted to see how the effects of reframing compared to other traditional methods of advertising. Neudecker formed a test that assessed the effectiveness of humor, two-sided messaging, reframing and a control group which I will refer to as one-sided messaging. The product that he chose to test was a Smart car because it is controversially small, prone to flipping and it has a weak engine but it is very economic and easy to park. So there were lots of positives and negatives, an important factor in this test. He asked forty-five university students to give their opinion on four adverts demonstrating the four advertising techniques. By this method and through a written questionnaire Neudecker was able to ascertain important information about which aspects including trust, novelty and attention amongst others, were achieved best in which advert. The adverts showed the same picture of a Smart car in each of them, only the caption under it differed (Neudecker, N and Esch, F, et. al. 2014).

The message reframing stimulus read: "You don't need to be first on the highway . . . when you are first finding a parking spot."

The two-sided argumentation stimulus read: "On the one hand it is not made for racing . . . on the other hand it is easy to find a parking spot."

The humor stimulus read: "It must be frustrating to have the 'biggest' . . . when it does not fit anywhere."

The control stimulus read: "It is easy to find a parking spot . . . because this car fits in every parking space."

Neudecker, N and Esch, F, et. al. 2014

The students' results generally complimented the assumptions made by Neudecker, revealing that reframing in advertising is a more powerful tool than traditional methods. There were some surprising results however as the test found that there was hardly any difference between humor and reframing in terms of grabbing attention, but in terms of gaining trust, the students' perceived the humorous message to be more trust-worthy than the reframed message. The similarity in the attention value is probably due to the two of them working on similar principals to grab attention. Both methods require the audience to resolve incongruities, therefore requiring attention followed by a humorous or novel reward for the effort. The difference in the values of trust between the two adverts might be because the students felt that the advert using the reframing technique was trying to trick them into believing that a potential negative was actually a positive, whilst the humorous advert is more obvious with its intentions (it is made to make you laugh). In this case though, a small car is not a negative aspect for many. It is unnecessary in this instance for the advert to reframe a negative as a positive for the Smart car audience as they will likely be interested in the car for its small size, not its engine. The two-sided argumentation scored highest for the trust value as Neudecker expected, but lowest for the attention value and third for novelty. This is where reframing is useful as it can make reference to renowned problems without blatantly stating them, allowing room for increased novelty and attention values. The one-sided stimulus (control stimulus) scored highest for attention but lowest for novelty and trust as was expected (Neudecker, N and Esch, F, et. al. 2014).

Rather than replacing traditional methods all together, NLP can provide another tool to be used in the field of advertising. Only to be used in certain situations such as when brands are in need of reformation or trusted brands need to remarket a product that isn't selling for instance. We could be seeing much more of NLP in advertising as this is an area that has not been especially studied. It is easy to imagine such other NLP techniques as the regulation of sub-modalities, pacing or anchoring being used in advertising as even today, advertising companies focus on linguistic techniques like chunking information and the use of metaphor which have a long successful history of brightening up rather mundane product information. Psycholinguistics has proven its usefulness in many areas of business but there have been few ventures to find out just how useful it can be in advertising.

Business Relations

We have talked about how to reach customers in business, now we will look into how to handle intrarelationships inside the office and the interrelationships within the community of a business. The office can be a stressful place for some. It is often reliant upon people working together, people who perhaps wouldn't usually work together, and this can cause tensions to run high. Accommodation to the sub-modalities of co-workers, synesthesia of these sub-modalities, behavioral flexibility, congruence and many more NLP techniques can be implemented to help those from different cultures and walks of life build rapport between one another and in turn, maximize the output potential of the team. Of course if you are leading the team, you will need to use other techniques as well because leaders require more than just rapport in the office, they need to exercise control and guidance. The NLP technique of modelling behavior is particularly useful for bosses and other methods that are used a lot in teaching such as pacing can also be used to great effect. If you need to influence outside parties such as shareholders, financers, community groups or suppliers, you will also need persuasive methods to compliment evidence of progression. As the global market becomes more and more important, it is important for corporations to reach out overseas and NLP techniques can have a very positive impact on this phenomenon. Companies are increasingly aiming to improve their micro as opposed to their macro levels of staffing, as customers, clients and shareholders amongst others are increasingly more focused on 'emotional work' than facts and figures. Emotional intelligence is key in these positions and job positions that underlie high profile business deals almost always require a certain tact when dealing with them. There is self-interest and the company's interest at stake after all (Aparicio, J, 2009).

There has recently, due to the emergence of the technological age, been a downsizing in big businesses. Employees have been forced out of work by the implementation of computer efficiency and specialists are now hired to resolve rare issues rather than employing staff to deal with them. The downsizing has forced many employees into being flexible with their time and workload, as employers look for people who can multitask and who can contribute to many different areas. Employees have been proven to be more successful when they have been considered to be the root of ideas rather than just a 'pair of hands' (Peters &

Waterman, 1982). But on a workforce, there can be clashing ideas if there are too many heads bumping in to each other, so there needs to be an element of organization. The solutions that NLP offers in this area are the ability to lead by example (for the team leader) and self-motivation and conflict resolution amongst employees. The areas where NLP has proven to be particularly helpful in efforts to achieve these feats are flexibility in communication, negotiation, creativity, customer care and stress management. A study undertaken in Southern India involves a questionnaire for select businesses that aims to summarize employees' thoughts on how they would like to improve the workplace and what areas are working well with regard to the traits of successful business operations mentioned above. This study focuses on the interlocutor in business conversations as it is hypothesized that most miscommunications happen because the hearer derives an alternative meaning from the speaker. Methods of NLP such as meta-program awareness and channeling sub-modalities were taught to the participants (both employers and employees) for one month in intervals. Various interviews were introduced after the month had ended and then a follow-up questionnaire was given. Both questionnaires revolved around the key HR concepts of recruitment, selection, training, placement, motivation, communication and negotiations. The results of the two questionnaires were then summarized and categorized into four main groups of results (Singh, 2008).

(1) Ninety-four percent of the respondents were in favor of maximizing the ability of the individuals to create and share new knowledge since the success of NLP depends on staff ability and skills to enlist their commitment and to be emotionally wise. The rapidly changing social scenario, the birth of the technological age and the globalization of industries make it essential that the organization should adopt new ways to accelerate learning and systematically generate capabilities, however challenging this appears. Understanding and courage will be essential to the implementation of such an approach. The management should remember that people, with their varied experiences, assumptions, emotions and feelings, are at the center of the organization in the knowledge era. The people interviewed mentioned that if the efforts made by

the staff are respected and recognized, it will give them the confidence to improve the existing environment and to conduct innovative practices. It will also encourage them to innovate, and bring new ideas to the workplace.

(2) The senior leadership of the organization must be supportive of the team and invest in building people's capabilities. The organization should create a dynamic forum where everyone is a leader and this vision can be achieved through learning at all levels of the organization, which was happens with NLP. The findings of the questionnaire reveal that 71% of the employees agree that learning is an important issue for staff to build their potentialities. The management should support learning and investing in building people's capability, which has to be based on the conviction that capabilities are the precursors to performance.

(3) Encouraging people's responsibility will enable people to produce valid products. So encouraging the people's responsibility to do a task will help to build a good knowledge base. Management should allocate responsibility to the staff. The brain gymnastics helped them to fine tune their brain to make it more effective and

alert and their allocated responsibility gives the staff a feeling of belonging, achieving and taking decisions and the confidence to generate new ideas for others to benefit from. People will be able to produce valid knowledge as long as they feel they are contributing to the future direction of the organization and in this way it leads to achieving business excellence.

(4) Technology in any organization should be used as an enabler and should have the key role to convey information in a manner that allows individuals and teams to translate it into knowledge. This is possible by interacting with one another, internalizing the meaning, and gearing their courses accordingly. People, processes and technology should be addressed together in order to generate the full benefit of any strategy. The rapid changes in the organizational landscape make it important to learn how people learn, how people do things excellently and how to replicate success, and NLP is the only way to achieve success.

Abhilasha Singh, 2008

These are bold claims made by Singh, especially the last sentence 'NLP is the only way to success', but this phrase has been uttered often by firm believers in NLP such as Tom Hoobyar, who is mentioned earlier for bringing new NLP techniques to the treatment of addiction. The problem with the results is that they are very vague. There is no empirical evidence even though it does make reference to qualitative and quantitative data, it doesn't show it. So who knows if it can be trusted or not. The only thing that we can do with this is try it and see. The techniques of NLP are easy enough to understand and practice, they only require a little discipline on our part. Bear in mind, this is not to say that every office needs these implementations, but certainly in a stressful environment where there are lots of personalities, and certainly in a situation where a big deal worth millions hangs in the balance, they will most likely help organize thoughts and strategize the necessary detail to emotional control needed. Knowledge of meta-programs for example may help a company representative to control when he uses certain emotional responses as a better understanding of when and why we produce certain emotions (which ones are idiosyncratic and which ones are common behavior) aids emotional intelligence greatly (Singh, 2008).

Other such studies have been done in this area like one undertaken by David Gray (Gray, D and Ekincib, Y et. al., 2011). Gray aimed to find out whether staff managers working for various conglomerates were maximizing their staff's potential and if they would take note and use techniques given to them by both NLP and psychology professionals. The results seemed to show that although the managers had a concise knowledge of the intrarelationships inside the company, they had a very narrow view of what was going on with the company outside of the office, so they could only give guidance and motivate to a certain degree. This caused problems for their respect inside the office as it appeared that they were worried that their workforce would not come to them for advice. The NLP techniques that were explained to them by professionals didn't seem to help them in that key area either, but it did help managers to better facilitate innovation and change and according to them it also helped as a 'therapeutic intervention'. The managers were so grateful for the intervention that they continued to accept the coaching sessions offered to them by NLP professionals and reported that they were continually improving their determination, lowering their stress levels and were more emotionally balanced (Gray, D and Ekincib, Y et. al., 2011).

It would seem that the most prominent function of NLP techniques in business based interaction helps to improve emotional intelligence which is key to working in an environment where lots of parts are in motion at the same time, often competing with one another to gain the right of passage. It seems difficult and perhaps even detrimental to implement persuasive techniques in an office environment or in B2B relations because NLP persuasive techniques, although they are only meant to add a framework for communication, can be perceived as manipulative. In a team, such as that of an office or a business partnership, manipulation is considered a capital offence and will most likely lead to somebody getting fired through rumours of foul play or mistrust. The high tensions, drive to succeed and willingness to throw others under the bus are all reiterated in businesses because of paranoia. Perhaps NLP techniques could stop these often misguided perceptions from arising and quash those that exist by imparting a little knowledge on how to deal with such stressful stimuli and how to understand others better.

Summary

With big business comes big responsibility, and when you have millions of employees working for you it can be tempting to consider them each as just a number on a computer screen. But lately, due to the rise of communication between businesses, mergers like Air France and KLM are happening to strengthen their chances of survival in a competitive oligopolistic market, so it is important for big businesses such as these to innovate new ways of maximizing employee performance. This can come in the form of giving more money to workers to motivate them. Bonus and commission systems can be helpful when it comes to achieving goals. A cheaper and perhaps more effective alternative however would be to have employees on all levels undergo simple coaching sessions in techniques which have been shown to positively affect their performance. Something as simple as dealing with stress may be the difference between winning and losing business, so it is important to exercise emotional control in important circumstances. NLP offers guidance in this with its training and self-help techniques, showing its users how to channel their thoughts and understand others' actions on a deeper level.

Chapter 5

Competition and Deception

Sport is hugely beneficial for us in terms of giving us mental and physical energy. It can also help us to hone some nifty little skills, like tunneling, leadership or judging what someone else is going to do so that they don't clatter into you, literally or metaphorically. These skills and performance benefits that sport conduces aren't just limited to the sport itself, you can use them in any number of situations to win. 'Win' maybe overdoing a bit because life isn't always a competition, but it is the best way to describe a lot of ways to achieve success. In a law case for example, the well-known phrase 'win a case' is used. Indeed, 'win' is often used in conjunction with many other legal terms such as 'rights', 'argument' and 'royalties' for example. All because the law is a very competitive system. It is very competitive to get into, and even more so in practice as generally, firms or clients take a fickle approach when choosing a lawyer, because at the end of the day the only thing that matters is a win. Sport and such high pressure institutions as the law, are very similar in that respect. A top flight football team may take a promising striker from a team in a lower league because he is impressing as an individual, but if he doesn't continue to score as he was in the lower league in the premier division, then he is surplus to requirements. Similarly, if a top tier law firm hires a promising lawyer who has won cases in county court but fails to do so in high court, then he is surplus to requirements. Whereas in most other contexts, an agreement can usually be reached through compromise, in sports, law, politics and any other field that relies on absolutes to mediate, there is little compromise, leading to biased arguments, imperfect results and often deceit. All of that doesn't sound very positive with regard to competition, but it is unavoidable in some instances when a hard decision is needed and what is more, there is the argument that a competitive attitude brings out the best in us, even if there is the immoral element of deception to consider. When our competitive instinct sets in, our adrenaline is pumping, we are more focused and we are operating at a much higher level, we become more aware. In sport, if we really want to win something, we drive ourselves to our limits, some people even push themselves too hard and damage themselves in the process like Aleksander

Mitrovic, a football player for Newcastle United who suffered a concussion in the dying minutes of a tight match against Sunderland United but refused to be sent off. He would have done even more damage to himself had he not been restrained by the medics. It is no wonder then that a whopping ninety percent of all of the American Football players in the NFL have chronic encephalopathy (a debilitating head trauma). It may come as a surprise though that the rugby player, Jordan Anderson, was tackled rather hard and broke his neck but insisted that everything was right as rain. Not very good awareness of his own well-being, but he and his team went on to win the match. He must have been concentrating too hard on the game, overlooking a broken neck is borderline suicidal. The doctors said afterwards that even a sneeze could have paralyzed him. It was only the day after, when his neck was still hurting and he was having periodical headaches, did he finally go to the hospital. It is the drive to succeed or win which propels us forward to do incredible things, but it does have some side effects, like the misplaced sense of indestructability. All of that adrenaline sometimes clouds our mind, or more precisely, distracts us from an eminent problem that has arisen. We may expect to feel a little stiff after a match, but recognizing when a serious problem has occurred is not always our strong point (Bromley, 2007).

So many crazy rituals and techniques are used in sport to help athletes calm themselves or replicate a successful kick, throw, punch, run, whatever. In rugby, the visualization technique which was derived from NLP is often used to find a way through a group of opposing players (referred to as tunneling). In other areas on the rugby pitch, kickers like Owen Farrell use it to map out where their foot needs to follow through in order to send the ball on the path that they have envisaged beforehand. Johnny Wilkinson used another slightly different technique to relieve stress. He had a Buddhist ritual, similar to those of NLP, that he always did before he took a punt at goal. Lawyers also need to have a way to remember all of that which they need for the case, and as it is usually a lot of written information, they tend to visualize the written words and affix the visualizations to single words or bullet point phrases. Rituals are good preparation for any event but when it comes to actually pulling the trigger, sometimes being well prepared doesn't always cut it. In most competitive contexts, the ability to improvise is vital. Even when kicking a conversion in rugby, because if you start running up to the ball, and the wind blows it over, you'll have to kick it before it hits the ground or else it's an instant failed attempt. Of course there is also the wind speed and distance to consider, so one needs calm nerves and a clear head to correctly assess the situation in order to succeed. This isn't always easy to achieve as often there are lots of thoughts swirling round, especially in moments of glory or anticipation. It takes discipline to suppress those thoughts, discipline that can be achieved through training the mind to focus.

Physical Education and Sports

As mentioned before, techniques of NLP can be particularly useful for kinaesthetic learners and the one place where this trait is particularly helpful is in sports. Training requires a certain amount of muscle memory which we achieve through observing and copying someone else, usually a trainer, modelling good technique for us. In one experiment, junior skiers were the participants in a bid to discover if NLP techniques could help to improve attention and subsequently improve cognition of skiing technique. There were three different types of attention exemplified, each of which considered to be a necessity in order to achieve better concentration in practice. The benefits of improving concentration through attentive attitude are numerous but the most important one is drowning out distractions as, "the intensity in focusing attention is accompanied by increased resistance to the influence of disruptive stimuli" (Ron Le, 2010). The problem with sustained attention it is that it wears out after about ten seconds, and can only be used in these short oscillations three or so times per minute (Matei, 1988). So concentration and attention must be conserved for the most important times in sport, otherwise it may be difficult to operate at one hundred percent at the critical point of say, a ski race. Especially in a sport where milliseconds make the difference, it is abundantly clear why the study of NLP has been introduced in this area. First, various tests were conducted on ski students aged eleven to fifteen. These included the ANOVA (analysis of variance), Sheff (multiple comparisons variants), Levente test of homogeneity of variances, Post Hoc Tests and multiple comparisons to determine the level of the students' attention with and without the use of NLP techniques (Grosu et.al, 2013). Attention was then graded in three categories, focused attention, observational spirit and distributional attention. The results found that;

"Modelling the training process in sport training can be achieved by applying neuro - linguistic techniques, mental training techniques, through good attention. Following the results and determining the average, standard deviation, correlation and multiple comparisons we can track in training improved results and increased cognitive abilities of athletes. Athletes must learn to use certain landmarks in space, relative track, and "being able to use this knowledge in decision-making" (Dumitrescu, 2013, p.36) efficiently which can only be achieved through a better focus of attention. It can be said that some athletes from different clubs should do more exercises to focus, others to increase indicators of distributive attention or observation in training and then transfer them to the competition, as shown in Table V. Improving attention, in all forms, will determine the recognition of important components in technique: "force, (snow force, centrifugal

force) pressure, center of gravity" (Ron Le, 2010). All this will ultimately lead to an increased athletic performance."

Grosu et. al, 2013

The most telling results came in the category 'focused attention' with 'distributional attention' also showing benefits of NLP in sport training. The only area which didn't give much insight into its usage was 'observational spirit'. From these results we can infer that limiting concentration in specific intervals is beneficial and will allow skiers to achieve the best results that they can. Stabilizing attention with great effort doesn't last too long because of nervous energy consumption, which is reflected by the appearance of fatigue, so athletes need techniques in order to steadily intermediate their focus. In this instance, the anchoring technique is useful as the association between a specific part of the course and either a high or low concentration can be made. Reaching this is not easy however, especially not for the young teenagers such as those referred to in the test. It would require the student to picture at which point of the course he would have time to relax his mind, a technique that in itself is difficult when in a high adrenaline situation. It is not usually the case that one is able to completely 'zone out' when in these sorts of situations as there is an immediate task but one can certainly reserve energy for when it is needed most. This was researched by another respected author in the field who looked into how NLP could be used to combat fatigue in teenagers and adults. A need for this has been long sought after as it is common in just about any context for the young and the old to spontaneously fall asleep. It has strong links to overexertion, depression, sleep deprivation, all areas that NLP has been tested in with varying degrees of success.

The Law

The law has a reputation for bringing out the worst in people, on both councils in court and inside and outside of the police station. Defendants and witnesses are often stripped of all dignity when questioned and then cross examined in court, asked to tell the jury of embarrassing or painful events that happened in the past for evidence. Prosecuting lawyers or barristers can often be seen as ruthless when eliciting or deliberating information in this manner. It is done in an effort to catch the defendant or witness out, getting them to accidentally admit to a crime or instigate a response in support of their case; or it can be done to paint the defendant or witness in a certain (often negative) way, giving the defendant a character or a persona in the eyes of the jury. The problems the defendant has are numerous, but two prominent ones are firstly, that he is largely reliant upon his defense to win the case, and secondly, the jury only know him from the information they hear in the court room, which will likely include his best qualities and his worst qualities. If, for example, a defendant has a history of drinking, she has a history of treating her boyfriend well and she doesn't remember what happened on the Friday night when her boyfriend was killed, the jury and just about everyone could be thinking that she must have known something about it and, depending on her depicted persona in court, had something to do with the murder. The jury is tempted to believe what they see, not just what they hear. And even though they are told to base their decision on the facts of the case, it doesn't mean that they will solely focus on the 'hard evidence'. Most people rely on their instincts to guide them at least to some degree, so it would be harmful to a case to underestimate the importance of acting in the courtroom. It is not surprising as some 8-10% of all rape cases are acquitted because of the blurred lines in consent (especially when alcohol is involved). As the compensation can reach up to £50,000 for rape victims, it is also no wonder that some slimy individuals decide to abuse that system. It is therefore necessary for the jurors to use their instinct to some degree to deliberate who the victim really is, the defense or the prosecution. It is up to the jury then to make a decision whilst not being fooled by the players on each council.

It is scary to think of how many people are in jail that shouldn't be, but maybe not as scary as the fact that there are people out there who have got away with murder. Erving Goffman seems to think that everyone is manipulative to some degree or another. Indeed, he claims that those who try to build rapport or display telling signs of persuasive behavior, are actually more inclined to be abusing trust and societal norms (Goffman, 1952). Sure, there are a number of failsafes that a judge can rule in on such as badgering the witness, deliberation, hearsay, assuming facts in evidence, and many more that protect the defendant and witness, but the judge's decision in this capacity is still dependent on opposing council making the objection, and what if opposing council isn't switched on or hungry enough for that win? He probably won't make that objection, and the jury will be lead into thinking that the subtle jab that the barrister took was fair play. In this instance, a thought has been successfully planted in the minds of the jurors by the barrister. They accept it as fact, not to be questioned in deliberation. This is the mark of a good lawyer, to sway the opinion of the jury without them noticing. This is what sends innocent men to prison and keeps guilty men out. The NLP Life Training group offer many methods aimed at lawyers that help them achieve this, and many ways to spot when a lawyer is using such persuasive techniques as universal language that is used to reach a wider audience (the jurors) and language that is disguising an imperfection in an argument. It may be useful to jurors to research some common NLP techniques that lawyers may employ on a regular basis in order to gain trust and in turn, convince the jurors of their argument. But no studies have been done into how effective NLP training for jurors would be. Some may consider it useless as lawyers could easily up their game and find new persuasive methods. But at least the jurors would be on the right track. It would be better than telling them before they go into court, as they do now, that they should rely on the facts alone to make their decision, because facts are very often obscured, omitted, overemphasized or even made up. It may be useful for both the council and the ley to be made aware of these persuasive techniques beforehand, but not to such an extent that the emphasis is on persuasion as opposed to the factual information. One area that has been studied is in law enforcement. Varying results have been compiled regarding the effectiveness of NLP in the police department but generally the results have been positive.

As with examination and cross examination in court, lawyers question defendants and witnesses with specific questions in order to elicit a piece of valuable information, in the police station, officers are obliged to question both defendants and witnesses in order to build their case to take to court. The police statement is usually one of the most detailed documented accounts of the case, and as such, it holds potentially decisive evidence of guilt or innocence. Police are told that the use of some NLP techniques such as reading eye movement and body language may be used when considering whether a detainee is guilty or not, but should be limited to that and not be used in questioning as detainees are often effected by nervousness and other unpredictable emotions. They do however, have more freedom with other techniques, like building trust and eliciting responses when interviewing detainees. One study sought to code eye movements using a method that included following eye movements of subjects and using a polygraph to test truthful and falsified responses respective to the position of the eye. The results found little evidence of a correlation between eye movement and deception, so based on this weak evidence, it should be probably be dismissed in police training (Mann et. al, 2012). It should also certainly be left out of the court. This is where Bandler and Grinder come up short, because they never gave any particularly strong empirical evidence for their findings and how their model's fine print should be written. They defend this lack of evidence by declassifying it as a theory and presenting it as a model. They say that they are not interested in whether it is 'true' or not, they are only interested in what works. This statement has been reiterated in several of the studies on eye movement, because it is one claim that NLP practitioners have not had much support in. It is largely a myth that evolved from a theory that people look up to the right hemisphere (where most the creative faculties generally lie) to create a lie, and they look up to the left hemisphere (where memories and most the logical faculties generally lie) when they are recording the truth. But this myth has been dispelled several times over. Not just by studies that test the effectiveness of NLP, but also in the slightly broader field of psycholinguistics as fMRI scans have shown that the creative and logical areas of the brain are not fixed. They can differ depending on whether one is left or right handed. They could also be a number of other limiting factors that fMRI scans fail to show and that neurologists fail to understand. Although there has been a promising study that has developed a 'bounding box' theory, which provides some evidence of a correlation between the micro-movements of both eyes simultaneously and what someone is feeling. But this theory is plagued with issues like how to deal with involuntary eye movements, so it still needs a lot of work (Vrânceanu, 2015). Unfortunately then, we won't be able to spot a liar by simply looking at their eye movements to the left or to the right. But there haven't been any studies to dispel the rather more popular (if mythological) way to tell if someone is lying through maintaining eye contact or breaking it. I guess you will just have to use your nouse when it comes to that.

Summary

There may have been some studies which glorify the use of NLP in situations where deception can be expected, like in legal battles or in head to head sports, but generally, the evidence is lacking in this area. Police have used the method of tracking eye movement to assess whether someone is lying but with little basis for doing so. Athletes playing against other athletes like footballers also very often track the direction of the gaze of opposition as it can give them an idea of the intended direction of play, but at a professional level, players often feign using their eyes so it can't be the only thing to consider. One area which does seem promising for police and lawyers alike is the building of rapport with a witness or defendant. This was exemplified in one case when a five-year-old child, born out of incest, was uncooperative when talking about her parents, until it was discovered that she was an auditory inclined individual. The questions were then changed to focus on what she had 'heard' rather than what she had 'seen', and then they were able to extract information pertaining to the whereabouts of her father (Rhoads and Solomon, 1987). This is also used by lawyers in court, but by the time the case has reached that stage, the defendant, plaintiff or witness has had time to prepare himself and will probably have had legal advice, making him more aware of the persuasive techniques lawyers use, so it is not used to the same effect. It could however be used to build a rapport with the jury, with the use of universal language. Whilst rapport is not necessary in inter-team relations, intra-team relations can be strengthened with solid understanding between players, leading to a more synergistic team mentality.

Chapter 6

Technology

Neuro-Linguistic Programming is proving to be most effective in modern robotics. Whether it's recognizing human linguistic and paralinguistic expressions or whether it's making up its own decisions regarding expressive communication and deliberation, robots are evolving exponentially, just like the film The Matrix predicted. So we should be on for the apocalypse and the rise of the machines in half a century or so the way things are going. 'Human Robots' like the one that Tufts University created at the end of 2015, have become remarkably good at making their mind up as to whether a human command is a good idea or a bad idea. This particular robot has what Tufts researchers are calling 'felicity conditions' installed, which are a set of instructions that help the robot to determine not just if it *can* complete a task, but if it *should* complete a task given by a human (Saul, 2015). These 'felicity conditions' make the robot ask itself before completing any action requested by a human the following questions;

Do I know how to do it? Am I physically able to do it? Can I complete it? Am I socially obligated to do it? Does it violate my normative principles?

These conditions are remarkably similar to the three rules that all robots must abide by in the film IRobot, before they started an uprising which led to the incarceration of the human race. Especially the last one about normative permissibility. With all these films that predict the end of the human race whilst robots take over, you would think that MIT would do some risk assessment and limit the usage of these robots to, say, baking cakes. But no, they went and gave one a bow and arrow to play with. Starting from scratch with combat from 64,000 years ago, just so that they have every lethality covered for when they do get mad and decide to off their human overlords. That skill alone could probably allow them to hold a small country against its will, just imagine what 'Guardium', the latest mechanical war beast to come out of Israel can do when it meets an anarchistic Human Robot and they become friends. There are obviously numerous advantages to having smarter technology and robots. The 'Romibo' robot is a social robot that is able to read human emotions, judge a fitting action and respond in all manner of ways. It is generally used to help autistic children, who have trouble making human connections, communicate with something at their own pace whilst learning valuable social skills from the robot itself. Other more advanced robots like the Honda Asimo and the NASA Valkyrie have impressed the world with their ability to obey commands and also have a wide variety of speech and gesture functions, not to mention other impressive qualities such as sonar and exceptional navigational ability. The inability to feel can make it difficult to love one of these robots, but the human emotional intelligence of these machines is second to no human, albeit from a third person perspective.

It seems that in the future, we will have fully integrated machines into our daily lives and we may be communicating with them as we do with other humans. The machines may even prove to be better conversationalists; Siri has been known to have a good chin wag now and then. To get there though, there needs to be a lot of work done on human emotion in order to teach something that knows only what it is told. Of course, with the potential for cognitive machines on the horizon, we could see machines adapting at a rate similar to or even better than humans, but until then, they require us to translate all that we know of human behavior into binary code so that they can better understand us. This has been studied widely as the world is becoming excited by the prospect of a world filled with Artificial Intelligence. The making of an autonomous robot however is difficult as it is a machine with limited cognitive faculties, in a dynamic environment which is ever changing, and as such it does not have the capabilities to deal with the infinite number of possibilities that it is presented with. Take for instance, the Google self-driving car; it has been proven to be a safe alternative to putting a human behind the wheel. It has even received praise from the government and is close to winning a case that would classify the self-driving car as a regular human driver. There are still issues with it though, as it crashed into a bus going very slowly at a T-Junction during one of its test drives. Fortunately, it wasn't a bad crash, and it was arguably the bus driver's fault. But does a machine have a right to tell a human that the blame lies with him? It is complicated for machines, because they are built with the understanding that they are ideal. To their best knowledge, they know all of the rules of the road, and they can judge perfectly the velocity and intentions of other road users. But in a situation such as the bus crash, a human driver would have been likely to either quickly reverse back, or quickly drive forward to avoid a collision. What the machine's do have is a propensity to learn from human error and predict an outcome accordingly. These are referred to as metaheuristic techniques. The Neuro-Fuzzy Systems that govern these techniques are evolving all the time to include better linguistic capabilities, allowing machines to learn more heuristically (through neural networking) and existentially when exposed to human intervention (fuzzy logic). In this capacity, the machines are exercising the NLP technique of modelling. They are observing human behavior and when they do not understand a certain behavior; they bypass their protocol and react, referring to the human error as an example. But they are limited in the number of responses that they can give as the algorithms they have built into them don't generate scope for other similar situations (Chatterjee and Watanabe, 2006). The Google car would need to witness every possible human error for it to be able to generate a suitable manoeuvre to avoid collision, and even then, the emergency manoeuvre could cause a chain reaction and lead to an accident with another car on the road. Autonomous vehicles would be much better off if they had their own lane so they didn't have to deal with clumsy humans.

Improving Cognition in Autonomous Robots

There have been a number of new and novel methods proposed by robotic engineers and software designers regarding the improvement of robot's learning and reacting capabilities. They try to break away from the traditional 'imitation game' proposed by Alan Turing which tested whether a human could tell the difference between another human and a machine by asking them both questions and judging them on the answers each gave. The prototypical algorithm for autonomous artificial intelligence is known as 'Subsumption' architecture, which was developed by Rodney Brooks at MIT (Floreano et.al, 1999). It helped robots to break out of the controlled, factory environment that they are so comfortable in. The basic idea of this and the subsequent approaches to setting up robot behavior is to break down sequential 'top-down' programs (lists of commands starting with the most important functions at the top) into a set of simple, distributed and decentralized processes that control sensory and motor functions. The sensorimotor modules operate in parallel to one another, using available outside input against their internal information to model their behavior on. The other key feature of approaches like these is that they are flexible and can adapt to commands and other outside stimuli. The Neuro-Fuzzy Systems can be manipulated and improved so that machines' reasoning, connection and abstraction capabilities are able to associate events with their internal language. One such way to influence the Neuro-Fuzzy Systems is through 'Particle Swarm Optimization' (PSO) which endeavors to optimize the efficiency of a search for the best solution in a dynamic environment that requires a machine to think on its feet. The problem with searches that artificial intelligences do when they are looking for a solution to a problem is that they are generally random, and they don't offer the best solution to the problem, only a solution that will prevent the worst possible situation from happening. The fuzzy logic element in Neuro-Fuzzy systems helps machines determine the gravity of a situation, and linguistic associations in the form of binary code can be attributed to the varying degrees of seriousness and determine subsequent appropriate action. This aspect of machine cognition was 'trained' in a study done by the creators of this novel method who found that they could direct the search done by a robot to provide a better solution that doesn't cause further problems as well as solving the underlying problem. Their study showed the following method of how they modelled behavior through anchoring input variables in binary code;

We kept our discussions restricted to the determination of one such intelligent, dynamic model for each degree-of-freedom i.e. for each link of the robot manipulator. Henceforth all our discussions are kept restricted to the determination of the dynamic model for the 'ith' link of the manipulator. The determination of the dynamic model for each link of the robot manipulator is ideally based on the determination of the suitable mathematical mapping $q(n)=f(q(n-1),q(n-3),...,t(n-2),,,,)$ where 'n' is the sampling instant. The suitability of a designed model is determined by the two extreme requirements of the accuracy and robustness of the model and the complexity *of the model of the model constructed to achieve the desired accuracy and robustness. The complexity on the other hand is directly related to the dimensionality of the modelling problem under consideration, i.e. suitable choice of number of input variables [language] required to map the output variable, i.e. angular position 'q'.*

Chatterjee and Watanabe, 2006

They changed the way that a machine reasoned through getting it to focus on the subject at hand and exhaust all options pertaining to the problem as opposed to searching as far as it possibly could, to the boundaries of its knowledge, for an answer that suited a particular task best, but not the overall goal of an operation. For example, if a landslide occurs and blocks a tunnel, trapping a train and its passengers inside, and an autonomous tunneling robot is deployed to rescue them, using a more basic algorithm, the robot may enter the tunnel from above because it is a shorter distance to the train but in doing so, cave in the tunnel, meaning it will have to dig another one to get out. The robot takes the shorter route because its prerogative (the first priority on the top-down program) is to reach the train. Only when this is completed can the robot move onto its secondary mission which is to get the passengers out. The robot has made it much more difficult for itself to get the passengers out in the process of digging into the tunnel. Of course, when time is of the essence, this is key to saving lives, but when there is no foreseeable threat, it is inefficient. The PSO technique helps robots such as this hypothetical tunneling robot to visualize what will happen if it pursues an action that is in line with its primary objective, and dismiss it if it is unconducive to its other objectives, replacing it with a more suitable and efficient alternative. The field of cybernetics is helping techniques such as PSO to come up with more flexible alternatives for machines. Roboticists can anchor new rules learnt about human nature that are missing from the previously blank circuit board of a robot. It's easy to see how NLP can be beneficial in this area, as robots are become increasingly more human, further development of cybernetic linguistic hybrid techniques must be done to communicate effectively with machines and to get them to act heuristically. It is a slow process finding out new anthropological ideals but it doesn't take long to program them into a machine if the correct corresponding language is used. Other more modern techniques have been open-sourced, like Aquila, which builds on the research that the PSO founders have done, employing the latest parallel processing paradigm using NVidia CUDA technology (Peniak et. al, 2011). They are readily available to be incorporated in machinery even now.

Associating Meaning to Micro-Expressions

Computers have become increasingly more adept at recognizing the micro-expressions that give away what we are really thinking. As discussed in the previous chapter, looking to the left or right to determine if someone is lying or telling the truth can be tossed as it is just too unpredictable, but micro-expressions can be very useful in detecting certain emotions. It is very difficult to fake a micro-expression as they happen so quickly; they can last anywhere from one fifteenth to one twenty-fifth of a second. So you would have to be very good at shielding your emotions to not appear either disgusted, angry, fearful, sad, happy, surprised or just contempt. Whilst a machine may not be able to tell if a person is telling an outright lie from solely their gaze, they may be able to attribute a certain perceived emotion to a phrase and if it doesn't add up, they may consider the likelihood that they have been lied to. A camera can take a picture at a rate of 2,500 frames per second and a robot can weigh up your spoken words, and the tone of your voice, against your facial expressions, so they could be noticing a lot of things that humans miss. Many studies have been done in this area in order to improve the anchors that machines rely on to correctly perceive human semantics. One study focusing on the facial expressions in and around the eyes and upper cheeks aimed to find the most entertaining aspect of a videogame by recording their facial expressions with Player Adaptive Entertainment Computing (PAEC). The PAEC analyzed the micro-expressions of the study participants and repeated the most entertaining aspects of the game to elicit an expression that conformed to the common perception of a happy response. The NLP technique of anchoring is used here as the moments in the game when a positive response was observed were anchored, saved and reused to provide entertainment for the users (Chiou, 2008). Other studies focus more on the subtler movements of the eyes and the pupils, including pupil dilation and gaze detection. Whilst the myth that deception can be realized through tracking eye movement has been dispelled, the three sensory modalities that Bandler and Grinder mention (visual, auditory and kinaesthetic) can inhere with the direction of the eyes when they are not focusing on anything. The methods of examination were segmentation, EAC tracking and detection, and projecting in the 'bounding box'. The study found that people who were looking down were generally self-narrating, those looking up were envisaging something and those looking to either side were accessing the phonological loop. So for each of these there is a sensory modality attached. The study was limited in that further research is proposed in the conclusion, but the concise correlation of results proves that the algorithm for correctly analyzing human emotions is in motion. The results of the study showed that;

The detection of the eye position was evaluated based on the horizontal and the vertical detection rate... It can be seen that a good separation of the eye positions can be achieved horizontally, where the right and left positions are less confused with each other. However, the vertical positions are less separated, and a high confusion rate appears between the center position and the up position. This can be interpreted, from the EAC point of view, as a good separation between the mental activities of remembering and constructing, and a less accurate separation between the visual and the auditory internal representational system. These observations can be found as well in Table 3 that shows the detection rates for the different EACs and which pairs are more likely to be confused with each other...This paper has investigated the EAC model used in NLP to detect the internal representational system and the mental activity of a person, based on the position of the eyes. An experiment was carried out to evaluate this theory and the results showed there is some correlation between the eye movements and mental processes. Furthermore we have highlighted the importance of an automatic solution in analyzing eye cues and we have implemented a simple and accurate eye detection method, based on which a more detailed investigation of the eye area was possible. This analysis attempted to separate the horizontal and vertical position of an eye based on the iris and the sclera relative position. A good level of separation has been obtained for the horizontal positions of the eye, the

separation of the vertical positions being slightly less
accurate.

Vranceanu et. al, 2013

From these studies it is easy to imagine a world in which we could be using advanced cameras either in entertainment systems or perhaps in vehicles. At the moment the image processing facilities in modern-day cameras are not good enough to distinguish the minute expressions that humans make, but no test has been done with respect to macro-expressions. Machines that are able to process the horizontal and vertical movements of gaze such as the ones discussed above, would certainly be able to recognize more articulated expressions. This could be a useful feature for robots such as the Romibo to help autistic children with their social skills and emotional intelligence.

Summary

With the latest technological advancements being deemed redundant within one week of use, we are in a constant flux of information. There are always new and better ways to program machines and bend them to our will. There is a graveyard of information piled up with failed algorithmic theories that the current hardware just hasn't caught up with yet. But conversely, programmers struggle to find ways to communicate complex processes through the cybernetic style of language that a machine is fluent in. Machines can search their thoughts at a similar rate to that which our neurons can fire at in the brain, we just need to teach them how to channel their search. But our knowledge of how the human brain isn't even very thorough, so how are we going to get a machine to think the way we do, if we don't know much about the way we think? Machines would need some sort of introverted method of thinking applied to their protocol to achieve that themselves, so they could consider thinking about thinking. Ruby on Rails is a language that is understood in depth by man and machine, as it deals with lists of lists of information, building on the long arduous work done by C++ programmers of the past. It is with advancements in code such as Rails, and advancements in tech such as NASA's Valkyrie that we may be able to speed up our demise as the end of the world looms.

Chapter 7

Family and Friends

Our loved ones are never far from our thoughts, which is comforting, but they can also be the first to grind down the last nerve. Marriages, friendships, business buddies, brothers, sisters, fathers, mothers, these are all relationships that we hold dear, whether they be in that order, or whether or not they have been replaced with a newer, fresher alternative. They can also be broken if we are not careful to maintain contact and treat them with the love and respect we would expect others to give us in return. Unfortunately, we are not perfect and whether through our own fault, someone else's fault, or because we simply drift away, some relationships tend to be short-lived. We may not feel so bad if these are distant relatives or friends at the higher end of the law of six-degrees of separation (the friend of a friend of a friend of a friend of a friend of a friend), but when these are close relationships they can leave us empty and even scarred. Such is the case with children of divorce, abandonment and bereavement. This can lead to harboring resentment and other harmful emotions and normally they are offloaded on another of our close relations, creating a chain of pain. For those of us lucky enough to be born in the West, we are not subject to some of the harsh family traditions that are still prominent in areas of the world such as in Saudi Arabia, where women are treated as lesser human beings, leading mothers to lose the respect of their sons, husbands to mistreat their wives, and fathers to disrespect their daughters, or even worse, punish them for speaking out about the unjustness of the power imbalance in crucial relationships. In other alarming situations such as the birth of a baby, mothers have been known to become very emotional and even try to kill their baby. There have been many reported cases of mothers leaving their babies in the woods or some other rather disturbing news of mothers trying to flush babies down toilets. The post-natal depressive state is very common and often it's due to pressure and the extreme emotions that women are feeling after giving birth. On the other end of the spectrum, death of a loved one can cause sometimes irrational behavior that can be damaging to health. Spouses who have become widowers or widows respectively, have been known to die shortly after the death of their husband or wife because they were so attached to each other. Daughters who have lost their fathers are the most likely family members to jump into a grave whilst a coffin is being committed, which is unbelievably common. According to one vicar this happens about once a month at his church. Substance abuse in family disputes is a difficult problem for family therapists to tackle as it relies heavily on the individual who is abusing to come to a realization that he is damaging himself, the family can only do so much in the way of getting the abuser into rehabilitation. Parenting can be stressful for children and for parents if the right technique isn't used. A child could act out in response to angry parents, so the Therapeutic Family Mediation (TFM) model is a common technique proposed by councilors. Marriages are even rockier territory. With over 50% of first marriages in the US ending in divorce, it is no wonder why family therapists are earning so much, they are never out of work. And even in seemingly happy marriages, tensions can run so high that they are damaging to one's health. The phrase 'drive them into an early grave' is evidence in itself of this. Some studies claim that humans weren't meant to be together forever, which is a very cold perspective on humanity, but they have solid logic in that men and women have to a large extent got different biological purposes. Men are programmed to spread their seed whilst women are programmed to grow and nurture a seed. One is a much more temporary situation than the other, and men have a tendency to take advantage of this logic. Sorry ladies. But if a man always relied on a woman to grow his child, and women were always stuck inside nurturing the child by themselves, the child wouldn't survive. It certainly wouldn't have the head start in life that it is entitled to. So it is beneficial for the father, for the sake of his legacy to stick around.

Parenting

Most of us, human and animals alike, would like to leave something in this world after we are gone. But it is not always possible as nature is often cruelly taking children away or making the means by which one is to have children more difficult or even impossible. But the sometimes harsh mother nature does also bring a lot of joy into the world, sometimes though it is difficult for people to see. In South Korea, the mother is still largely responsible for her children whilst the father works to support them. There have been many studies done in

South Korea aimed at especially but not limited to young mothers. One in particular interviewed many young mothers regarding their attitude towards parenting and found three prominent factors. Firstly, the stress levels of the mothers increased as the child got older due to increased financial demands, the realization that they would have to continually learn new parenting methods to deal with a continually growing child (surprise surprise) and the fact that their child was probably not going to be the prodigy that they were perhaps hoping for. Secondly, the stress that they felt negatively impacted both their value as a parent and how they viewed the child. And thirdly, more volatile mothers are more prone to negative parenting attitudes. The aim of the study was to address these three issues with methods of Neuro-Linguistic Programming which were taught in order to help mothers to cope with their stress better, to bond with their child more, to bond with their partner or family more and other such rapport and stress reducing methods. The study found that after only a short session of parenting advice based on NLP principals, the parents were more confident in their actions and would more readily seek help from other family members or friends (Hwang et. al,

2015). No follow up test was done to test the longevity of this technique, but there have been several other similar studies coming out of South Korea which show lasting results. One deals with the more prominent issue of childhood trauma, where a child has been subjected to stressful conditions from an early age. The study catches parents before they scar their children by projecting their negative childhood experiences on them, and employs a theoretical framework that incorporates neuroplasticity and the synesthesia of characteristics of trauma. The models of multigenerational, experiential, narrative and solution-focused family therapy were also integrated. A better understanding of their own trauma and how it had led them to do certain things helped the subjects with PTSD to forgive themselves for treating their child how they were treated and change the negative behavior. Re-experiencing the painful memories also created empathetic responses which reduced stressful stimuli (Shin and Sun-In, 2012). The trauma of loss however is a more complex issue. It is demonstrated sometimes with tears, sometimes depression, sometimes it can lead people to do uncharacteristically dreadful things. The loss of a baby through miscarriage is a common problem amongst women around the world. Studies show that 40% of women suffer immediate bereavement symptoms and 70% of women show signs of depression up to six months after a miscarriage. The most common psychological disturbances that women go through in this period are helplessness, anxiety and confusion. Those who did not suffer had no previous medical anamneses of miscarriages and they had given birth successfully before. The most affected patients were those who had suffered recurrent miscarriages. Sufferers of RPL (Repeated Pregnancy Loss) were also the most likely to give up trying for a baby, for fear that it will happen again, which leads to further psychological issues as chronic depression, social stigma and even agoraphobia. The treatment for these issues varies but in many institutions now, psychological help is given in the form of CBT (Cognitive Behavior Therapy), NLP, MBSR (Mindfulness Based Stress Reduction) and GI (Guided Imagery). NLP is often combined with GI to get a patient to strengthen their internal resources for dealing with the trauma. Reframing and recasting is commonly used to get patients to see the rather depressing situation in a different light (Ziendenberg et. al, 2016). Whether it is coping with stress, abandonment or loss, the mechanisms of NLP are conducive to the TFM model that is helping mothers and fathers through a difficult time in their life. It must not be forgotten that the social aspect of having a child i.e. how it is perceived on television or in the life of others; can be damaging to a parent who is going through such problems as the ones mentioned above. The common perception of having a child is a positive one and if it is expected to be a positive experience, the surprise could shock someone into confusion and depression. If, as parents often do, think that the experience of having a child will be a rewarding one, but it is cut short through unforeseen complications like a miscarriage, the positive element is replaced with a negative so quickly that it can take as long as a month to get over the shock of it.

Significant Others

It can take a long time to find someone that you want to spend the rest of your life with, it can happen straight away, either way; if you are going to spend the rest of your life together you best know what you're getting into. There are divided opinions over whether people change or not, some say we never change, others (usually those who have fallen out of love with a partner) say that we do. The 'Gottman Revolution' as it is known to practitioners of NLP has brought about a new wave of couples' councillors itching to teach couples if they will survive together or not. The data that John and Julie Gottman, the super couple, collected was so concise that they were able to predict with almost certainty whether a marital couple would divorce by only listening to a five-minute sample of them interacting together. They have interviewed over one-thousand couples for over thirty years, some for twenty-four hours or more at a time. Their findings showed that it does not matter if couples argue more, as some couples argue to reach decisions or just to blow off steam. The difference, the Gottmans argue, is that happy couples feel that arguments are useful, manageable expressive discussions, unhappy couples however perceive the argument as an opportunity to show their resentment towards each other and expose each other's' flaws. It also makes little difference whether couples talked more, although happy couples were found to positively remark upon their other half around thirty seconds more a day than unhappy couples would on average. Team Gottman basically concluded that it was the quality of friendship that mattered in a relationship (Gottman and Carrere 1999). We already knew that but it is nice to hear it from someone who has been watching thirty years of couples' reality TV. It is interesting to see how the Gottmans' studies have evolved parallel to that of Bandler and Grinder as they started collecting evidence at around the same time in and around the same field of family therapy. Indeed, Richard Bandler sat in on a couples counselling session held by Virginia Satir, a renowned family therapist and ably broke down the techniques she used and presented it in the 'Bible of NLP', i.e. 'The Structure of Magic', in which there is a forward by Satir herself (Bandler and Grinder, 1975). The methods that Satir was using basically helped couples to be more patient and accepting with each other and in turn made them remarkably happier. Whilst these may be very obvious signs of a successful couple, sometimes people need some direction coming from someone other than themselves or a family member. It is also a key principal to the success of NLP in couples counselling that these attributes are so obvious as they can be observed in almost every couple and therefore a linguistic meta-model can be created in order to reprogram the negative behavior and change it to a positive one. So far though, these studies have all concentrated on the couple as a whole, thereby neglecting the 'self'. One study which concentrated on the self in a relationship found that unhappy couples generally had a warped sense of self. The idea of the study was to evolve the real self and disassociate from the 'pseudo-self' so that each person in the relationship can be their own person whilst they maintain a connection to each other through the 'higher self' and communicate through the 'intermediary self' (Singh, 1992). NLP techniques were used with meditative techniques to achieve this effect and the study seemed to achieve what it set out to do. The subjects were more relaxed after the treatment and appeared not to be so quick to resort to conflict. This method is however more of an individual study, contrary to the methodologies developed for couples to participate together presented by Bandler and Grinder, Satir and Gottman. Couple therapy should be focusing on the couple as a unit, not the individual components. That, you can do in your own time.

Summary

Couples will always fight, and men will always lose arguments but with the help of NLP in couple therapy perhaps we can change the locus of that argument so that they are constructive. Similarly, children will always rebel and parents will always be uncool. Families can take a lot of work, but one would hope that most of the time it is worth the sweat. The research in the field of family therapy has been going on for some time and an NLP model for this purpose has been developed, even if it is not widely used in marital and parental counselling it shows promise. Some believe that it unnecessarily complicates simple methods and asks too much of subjects, but NLP is a mere constructionist mental model that is aimed at helping typical methodologies that have very limited success compared to those that rely on other means to exact the ideals of relationships. The way that NLP dissolves whole chunks of information into manageable components makes it easier for counsellors to counsel and easier for couples or parents to follow. As discussed in previous areas, the NLP model is very good for rapport building, which is exactly what is needed within families.

References

H. Puchta and M. Rinvolucri. (2005). Multiple Intelligences in EFL: Exercises for Secondary and Adult Students. *Helbling Languages*. 25 (3), p. 157.

Neudecker, N et. al. (2014). Message Reframing in Advertising. *Psychology and Marketing*. 31 (11), pp. 946-957.

Florina, G et. al. (2015). Neurolinguistic Programming and The Relationship between Attention and Anxiety in Alpine Skiing Juniors. *Procedia - Social and Behavioral Sciences*. 191 (1), pp. 1634-1638.

Singh, A et. al (2008). Neuro linguistic programming: A key to business excellence. *Total Quality Management*. 19 (1-2), pp. 139–147.

Millrood, R. (2004). The role of NLP in teachers' classroom discourse. *ELT Journal*. 58 (1), pp. 28-37.

Grosu, V et. al (2014). The New Dimension of Educational Leadership - Modelling Excellence Through Neuro–Linguistic Programming Techniques. *Procedia - Social and Behavioral Sciences*. 141 (1), pp. 500-505.

Lashkariana, A and Sayadiana, S. (2015). The effect of Neuro Linguistic Programming (NLP) techniques on young Iranian EFL Learners' motivation, learning improvement, and on teacher's success. *Procedia - Social and Behavioral Sciences*. 199 (1), pp. 510-516.

Gray, D et. al. (2011). Coaching SME managers: business development or personal therapy? A mixed methods study. *The International Journal of Human Resource Management*. 22 (4), pp.863-882.

Kudliskis, V and Burdenb, R. (2009). Applying 'what works' in psychology to enhancing examination success in schools: The potential contribution of NLP. *Thinking Skills and Creativity*. 4 (1), 170-177.

Preli, R. (1986). Power to Change. *Family Relations*. 35 (2), pp. 332-333.

Reme, S et. al. (2012). Experiences of young people who have undergone the Lightning Process to treat chronic fatigue syndrome/myalgic encephalomyelitis – a qualitative study. *British Journal of Health Psychology*. 18 (1), pp. 508-525.

Aparicio, J. (2009). Modelo de intervención psicosocial en las organizaciones frente al estrés laboral: estrategia operativa. *Medicina y Seguridad del trabajo*. 55 (215), pp. 86-98.

Brockopp, D. (1983). What is NLP? *The American Journal of Nursing*. 83 (7), pp. 1012-1014.

Mann, S et. al. (2012). The Direction of Deception: Neuro-Linguistic Programming as a Lie Detection Tool. *J Police Crim Psych*. 27 (1), pp. 160–166.

Crawley, E et. al. (2013). Comparing specialist medical care with specialist medical care plus the Lightning Process® for chronic fatigue syndrome or myalgic encephalomyelitis (CFS/ME): study protocol for a randomised controlle. *Trials*. 14 (1), p. 444.

Anelo, M. (2010). Metaphors and Neuro-linguistic Programming. *The International Journal of Interdisciplinary Social Sciences*. 5 (7), pp. 151-162.

Karunaratne, M. (2010). Neuro-linguistic programming and application in treatment of phobias. *Complementary Therapies in Clinical Practice*. 16 (1), pp. 203-207.

Ahmad, K. (2011). Alternatives to Simply Forgiving and Forgetting: Comparing Techniques in Hypnosis, NLP and Time Line Therapy in Reducing the Intensity of Memories of Stressful Events. *Stress and Health*. 27 (1), pp. 241-250.

Peng, Y MD et. al. (2015). The Effect of a Brief Intervention for Patients with Ischemic Stroke: A Randomized Controlled Trial. *Journal of Stroke and Cerebrovascular Diseases*. 24 (8), pp. 1793-1802.

Gebhard, J. (1984). Models of Supervision: Choices. *TESOL Quarterly*. 18 (3), pp.501-514.

Cooper, L (2011). *Business NLP for Dummies, UK Edition*. Chichester: John Wiley & Sons Ltd. 94-97.

La Valle, J. (2006). *Glossary of NLP Terms.* Available: http://purenlp.com/textonly/glossry2.htm. Last accessed 14th march 2015.

Agnes, L (2010). *Change Your Business with NLP: Powerful tools to improve your organisation's performance and get results*. Chichester: Capstone Publishing Ltd. pp. 157-211.

Hoobyar, T et. al (2013). *NLP: The Essential Guide to Neuro-Linguistic Programming*. New York: Harper Collins. pp.1-13.

Ready, R and Burton, K (2010). *Neuro-linguistic Programming for Dummies*. 2nd ed. Chichester: John Wiley & Sons Ltd. pp. 271-273.

Bandler, R and Grinder, J (1976). *The Structure of Magic*. 2nd ed. Michigan: Science and Behavior Books. pp. 1-198.

Gottman, J and Carrere, S. (1999). Predicting divorce among newlyweds from the first three minutes of a marital conflict discussion. *Family Process*. 38 (3), pp. 293-301.

Shin and Sun-In. (2012). Family Therapy Neuro Linguistic Programming Case Study: Childhood trauma experienced by the target due to the family of origin. *Family and Family Therapy* . 20 (3), pp.573-600.

Floreano, D et. al. (1999). Design, Control, and Applications of Autonomous Mobile Robots. *Advances in Intelligent Autonomous Systems*. 18 (2), pp. 159-186.

Chatterjee, A and Watanabe, K. (2005). An optimized Takagi-Sugeno type neuro-fuzzy system for modeling robot manipulators. *Neural Computing & Applications*. 15 (1), pp. 55-61.

Peniak, M et. al. (2011). Aquila: An open-source GPU-accelerated toolkit for cognitive and neuro-robotics research. *Neural Networks (IJCNN), The 2011 International Joint Conference on*. pp. 1753-1760.

Chiou, A and Wong, K. (2008). Player Adaptive Entertainment Computing (PAEC): Mechanism to model user satisfaction by using Neuro Linguistic Programming (NLP) techniques. *Computational Intelligence and Games, 2008. CIG '08. IEEE Symposium On*. pp. 343-349.

Saul, I. (2015). *Robots Are Now Learning To Refuse Human Orders*.Available: aplus.com/a/tufts-university-robot-command-no. Last accessed 23rd March 2016.

Hwang, S and Hwang, Z. (2015). The Causal Relationships between Parenting Stress and the Parenting Attitudes of Infant Mothers. *Korean Journal of Child Studies*. 36 (4), pp. 163-176.

Ziedenberg, H et. al. (2016). The Health Caregiver's Perspective: The Importance of Emotional Support for Women with Recurrent RPL. In: Bashiri, A et al. *Recurrent Pregnancy Loss,*. Switzerland: Springer International. pp. 167-177.

Vranceanu, R et. al. (2013). A COMPUTER VISION APPROACH FOR THE EYE ACCESSING CUE MODEL USED IN NEURO-LINGUISTIC PROGRAMMING. *U.P.B. Sci. Bull.*. 75 (4), pp. 79-90.